"For God alone, O my soul, wait in silence."
—Psalm 62:5 (ESV)

3rd Edition

WAITING
ON
GOD

A 31-Day Adventure into the Heart of God

A N D R E W   M U R R A Y

IGNITING
PRAYER
ACTION

The Woodlands, Texas

Waiting on God
A 31-Day Adventure into the Heart of God – *3rd Edition*
by Andrew Murray

Copyright © 2019, 2020, 2022 Igniting Prayer Action

Updated in modern English, 2020
Previously published by Igniting Prayer Action as *Waiting on God:
A 31-Day Journey Into God's Word on Prayer and Waiting on God*, 2019

Edited and updated by Jennifer Huber
Cover and page design by Justin Boland

For special print orders for your church or ministry, email us at
colin@ignitingprayeraction.org or write to us at the address provided below.

Published by Igniting Prayer Action
P.O. Box 132861
The Woodlands, Texas 77393

Printed in The United States of America by
Disc Pro Graphics & Printing, Houston, Texas

ISBN: 9798358515963

Contents

Foreword 2022
126 Years Later

By fellow South African Colin Millar
President of Igniting Prayer Action

Precious friend-in-Jesus,

This is our third edition of *Waiting on God*. In the past two years God has exploded His commanded blessings through tens of thousands of lives in multiple nations through the life-transforming training in Waiting on God and Luke 10 Transformation. The following are just some of those amazing results.

In June 2021 a team of us Zoom-trained 116 leaders from eight nations in Waiting on God and Luke 10 Transformation. This exact training is also available to you at: www.ignitingprayeraction.org/l10tvideos/

Bishop Evariste Harerimana in Burundi and Pastor Baluki Napoleon (his disciple and now our spiritually adopted son) in DR Congo then trained over 2,000 men, women, and children. Together they are bearing much fruit through two multiplying disciple and church planting movements in both Burundi and DR Congo, yielding over 4,000 new multiplying disciples and 25 new church plants. In June 2022 another 195 multiplying disciples became a fourth generation in this movement.

Since January 3, 2022, through the Greater Houston Prayer Council (www.ghpc.us), founded by my long time friend Pastor Rickie Bradshaw an average of 55 of us have met online by Zoom from 6:00 to 7:00 a.m. every morning without interruption! Today (September 9, 2022), marks the 244th day in which we have read the day's meditation together, then waited in silence (often for 15 minutes), prayed and share amazing testimonies. As the days went by, we watched God restore marriages and heal sibling/children/grandchildren relationships. We experienced deep renewals of joy, peace, and passion to serve with loving, tender excellence in our families, in our places of work, wherever and whenever we would go.

You will read testimonies from just a few others at the back of this book; however, my passionate encouragement to you remains the same.

Please read and then PRACTICE what you read in this book, and you will encounter the presence of God so personally you will never be the same.

I have read, taught from and promoted Andrew Murray's books for the past 32 years. God has used his *Abide in Christ, Humility, With Christ in the School of Prayer* and others to significantly challenge and grow me in my personal relationship and prayer life with God.

Then I discovered this little book you are holding in your hands! Over the past two years as I have read, learned, grown but most importantly PRACTICED this simple, but not easy, art and discipline of waiting on God, several things have become very apparent:

• I am encountering the simple yet overwhelming joy and peace of our Father to a hugely greater extent than ever in my 35 years of walking in a personal love relationship with God. For those of you who don't know me, my joy levels in Jesus are pretty high 98 percent of the time (just ask my beautiful bride).

- I am hearing and acting on an ever-clearer whisper of God's voice in my heart. He is even giving me answers to prayers I have never even prayed.

- I have taken Andrew Murray's quote literally: "A minister has no more solemn duty than to teach people to wait upon God." Together with a growing team in 5 nations 15,000 Waiting on God books have been printed and distributed and we are just printing 5,000 of our new "3rd" edition in English. Please pray for a new movement in Pakistan where partners Tahseer and Saba have translated the book into Urdu, our 4th language, with 5,000 copies being printed and distributed in this last quarter of 2022.

Our prayer is that you would join with thousands of other Christians who have heeded the call to wait on God.

Before we go any further, come with me onto the practice fields that are white unto harvest.

PRAY NOW with me:
"Father, please give me grace to wait, to be still, to sit quietly, stopping my racing mind and churning emotions so that I might just enjoy Your presence, right now for 5 minutes....(set a timer for 5 minutes and wait silently before God.) Tha   nk you, Jesus. Amen."

Sweet Saint, taking 5 minutes to be still with the Most High God (Psalm 46:10) is what I call a "Wait Five." This being still, declaring your absolute trust and dependence upon God only, is the very heart and core of what it means to wait on God.

Please read no further until you have done a "Wait Five." If, even my kindergarteners can do this, so can you!

PRAY NOW again:

"Father, as I delve into the pages of *Waiting on God*, would You teach me to wait on You? Would You give me grace to wait both patiently and yet expectantly, believing that You, the King of kings, are in this moment waiting on me to be gracious to me! (Isaiah 30:18) Would You remind me of forgotten dreams, unanswered prayers, challenging relationship issues with which You want me to trust You absolutely, once again. Oh yes, Lord, give me faith to believe, as Your Word says: 'How blessed are ALL those who wait on You!'"

Waiting on God Walking with Jesus
Fueled by the teaching of
Luke 10 Transformation

The 31 days of *Waiting on God* by Andrew Murray allowed us to experience the wonder of and different facets of waiting on God. The believer might wonder how the practice of waiting on God can be integrated into a lifestyle of following Jesus.

Luke 10 Transformation (L-10-T) is a course that shows a way to help every believer live a lifestyle of Christian discipleship and personal evangelism. L-10-T is based on the example of how Jesus sent out the 72 disciples in Luke 10:1-24. It seeks to equip every believer to live as His witnesses every day. Luke 10 records Jesus' instructions to His disciples back then, instructions that still show us today how disciples should live as His witnesses. In other words, personal evangelism and discipleship is God's ultimate way for believers to share Jesus with others.

From the South African birth of the L-10-T movement, it continues to grow currently in 43 nations teaching the way in four steps that every believer can follow:

1. to **Pray** every day for all;
2. to **Connect** with people around us, especially those who don't yet know Christ as Lord and Savior;
3. to **Care** for people with needs around us by assisting, encouraging, or praying;
4. to **Share** the gospel of Jesus as Savior with people around us. The L-10-T course assists believers of all Christian denominations to live a lifestyle that transforms themselves and their communities for Christ.

In 2020 Colin Millar of IPA (Igniting Prayer Action) and Willem Joubert (part of the original 2003 L-10-T development team) collaborated to integrate the principles of Waiting on God into L-10-T. We did it after waiting on God for His guidance in the entire project. The result amazed us and put the L-10-T course on a total new level. This is what we are sharing with you in this section. Let us first look at what L-10-T is.

What is so unique about the L-10-T lifestyle of following Jesus as His disciple?

Luke 10 Transformation takes EVERY believer from their current state of following Jesus and, in an easy way, lifts them to another higher or more expansive level of following Jesus with great joy! For example:

- **L-10-T helps believers who evangelize easily** -- This 4% of believers in the average church feel they increase their impact 8-fold after implementing L-10-T (from a study with 140 evangelists).

- **L-10-T equips the other believers** -- The 96% of believers in the average church who do not evangelize easily are shown how to be evangelists every day everywhere they are or go.

- **L-10-T offers training for all ages** – Adults and youth can do L-10-T. Even children from ages 4-14 can do L-10-T, as well as older, retired believers and families.

- **L-10-T is for every day** – In contrast to doing prayer, connecting with not-yet-believers, caring for the needy, and sharing Jesus once a week, once a month, or once a year, L-10-T allows the believer to do these actions daily.

- **L-10-T is for everywhere** – Believers can do L-10-T everywhere they move during any day of the week. For instance, they can do it while walking, cycling, shopping, playing, visiting, at work, on vacation, and more!

- **L-10-T is for all personalities and giftings** – People with different personalities can apply L-10-T just as effectively. Whether you're an introvert or extrovert, even people with various intelligence levels and other giftings (practical people, dreamers, worshipers, innovators, artists, managers, entrepreneurs, organizers, etc.) can all live the L-10-T lifestyle.

- **L-10-T can be done in different modes** – Parts of L-10-T are done silently (such as silent prayer with eyes wide open or waiting on the Lord). At other times, you may be talking and connecting or assisting others by using your practical skills.

- **L-10-T can be utilized at your workplace** – You can apply L-10-T either silently or more openly, as the situation or management allows, in your work environment.

- **L-10-T removes the Sunday/weekday divide** – Whether a church leader or a congregant, every day becomes a day of ministry for every believer.

- **L-10-T has no size limits** – While the training typically aims towards individuals; you may also precisely and powerfully utilize it for organizations or cities.

- **L-10-T is best when it becomes your lifestyle**

– The L-10-T training assists every believer to adopt the Luke 10 way of following Jesus.

- **L-10-T training compels users to become trainers** – As you begin applying the concepts, you are immediately challenged to train others to do L-10-T. This multiplication of disciples who are trained to make disciples may happen in your family, homegroup, workgroup, church, short-term mission, daughter church, denomination, city, town, region, or country.

Is Luke 10 Transformation or L-10-T for you?

L-10-T is a life-transforming curriculum designed to help you live out the call of the great commission to become a disciple who makes disciples. In doing so, you're sharing Jesus with others, even if they only see Him in you, and fulfill that call to personal evangelism. Overall, we designed this curriculum to make it easy for every believer to live it every day and everywhere.

Luke 10 Transformation is also the foundational tool for our discipleship training. The curriculum focuses on four simple but transforming steps. The beauty is you don't need to have a specific personality to share your faith with others; everyone can do this!

There are 4 steps that will now be explained in summarized form. We also explain how the practice of Waiting on God is integrated in each step.

Step 1: Pray for God's blessings.

Whether you're on a walk in your neighborhood, completing tasks at work, or shopping at the grocery store, Pray Now! Specifically, pray for God's blessings to be on people, businesses, communities, local churches, and wherever you go. Also pray for God's blessing on the tasks that you do. Praying doesn't require you to talk to anyone but God about what you see and experience daily, so you will mostly do it silently and with open eyes. Any believer can do this!

Waiting on God integrated into Step 1

Before integrating Waiting on God, prayer in Step 1 consisted of asking God to bless and assist in various ways. Now we ask L-10-Ters to wait for one to five minutes after they have prayed for someone, someplace, or a task. We call this short time of waiting on God during the day **Wait Five**.

> **Example:** While commuting one day, I saw a man walking. Although I did not know him, I did L-10-T Step 1 and prayed silently that the Lord would bless him fully. I concluded in the Name of Jesus and Amen. [**Explanation:** What I did was to act in the New Covenant role that every believer has, namely as a royal priest of the Most High (1 Peter 2:4-10). I asked God to bless that man in the fullest way that God would at that moment, believing that God would act at the right time to put His Name on that man (Numbers 6:27), even lead him to salvation if he did not yet know Jesus as Savior.] In the moments after that I then became quiet before God and just waited on God for a Wait Five moment for that man. [**Explanation:** I talked to God about showering him with His best. Then I became quiet and waited. Because God would know what was best for that man

at that moment, I might receive a wonderful peace from the Lord (Day 25) or I might receive instructions (Day 5). The instructions might be to go and talk to him or to pray more deeply for him.]

By doing Step 1 in this way we are fulfilling the Second Great Commandment to love others. And by praying and waiting, we are fulfilling the First Great Commandment to love God. We can also know that when we ask God to bless others, God will also bless us: *"Blessed are all those who wait for Him"* (Isaiah 30:18, Day 22). Furthermore, how do we know if God did not **wait on us**, to pray and wait on Him for that person (Day 20).

The 5 Levels in Step 1
There are five levels of doing Step 1 of L-10-T. Parts of the first level are described above. The other levels involve:

Level 2: Forgive those who wronged you or those close to you, currently or in the past and then ask God to bless them fully.

Level 3: Show appreciation to those around you for doing good by speaking words of affirmation or by deeds of service, giving of your time to be with them or small gifts or appropriate touch.

Level 4: Imitate the blessing of God's generosity by giving freely what you can: your money, your time, your skills or gifts, your love, or your possessions.

Level 5: Be a blessing by God's grace to those around you every day.

In Levels 2-5, combine Wait Five richly into the actions you take and for the people with whom you interact.

Step 2: Build relationships and make connections.

Build relationships with people you know who don't already have a relationship with Jesus Christ or who aren't actively living out their faith. Make a list of people with whom you would like to be intentional about developing a deeper Christian relationship. These people can be coworkers, people in your environment, or neighbors. Do ensure they are people with whom you have some existing connection, even if it is just knowing their name or face. As you may not have an existing relationship with these people, you will most likely target at least one not-yet-believer in this way.

Begin praying for the people on your list daily and ask God how to start the process of building a deeper relationship with them. As you connect with these people, visit them, eat and drink with them, and genuinely get to know their stories. In Step 2 you are drawing them closer to Jesus simply by their getting to connect with a believer. You are not obligated to talk about Jesus, unless asked. They should see Jesus in you.

Do not neglect any moments of connection you have with **other** people daily. Make every connection count – whether it is within or outside the family, with people you know or as a chance connection, like with a cashier at a till. It does not matter whether your connection is with believers, not-yet-believers, or people of unknown religious persuasion. We make connections count by being friendly, gracious, loving, peaceful, and by displaying the fruit of the Holy Spirit.

The other side of the coin of Step 2 is to make sure that there is no behavior in your life that would drive people around you away from Christ if they knew that you were a believer. Behaviors like loosing your temper, being arrogant, lying, stealing, being dishonest as an employee or as an employer could drive people away from Christ. Try to eliminate any bad behaviors by identifying them and then asking God or trusted advisors/counselors to assist. Such behaviors stand in your way to be an evangelist every day everywhere.

Waiting on God integrated into Step 2
In building relationships with people or just connecting with them on a regular basis, we always included doing Step 1 – praying for God's blessing on them. But now, we add another dimension to our relationships and connections when we Wait Five for them whenever we can.

> **Example:** As part of Step 2 I have identified X, a Hindu at my workplace, as a person that I will target to build a relationship with. While I have been praying for the Lord to bless him fully, I now grab a few minutes at various times during the day to lift X before God and just wait on Him. It brings a new depth to my relationship with X and with God.

> **Example:** Regarding any bad habit or sin in your life that might repel people around you from Jesus if they knew you were a Christian, you can now add Waiting on God about a sticky bad habit or sin to your arsenal of actions (Day 12). Many times, it is a new experience to wait on a just God (Day 19) about a sin in our lives, enlisting His help to get rid of it (Day 7).

Step 3: Care for people by helping with needs.

As you meet people in daily life and connect with them,

God and/or the people will begin revealing their needs to you. As needs are revealed, you should care for the people by doing something about those needs, or by encouraging them, or by praying to God that He will bring a solution to a problem. You may find that sometimes you do not hear about the needs people around you have. The easiest way to solve this problem is to ask someone the PRAY NOW question: "Is there anything that I can PRAY NOW for you personally?" People will often share their most pressing need in that moment, then you can either do something, encourage them, or pray with them.

The wonderful thing is that you may also care in the same way about the needs of organizations or groups of people.

Waiting on God integrated into Step 3
As believers hear about the needs of people around them, we now encourage them to Wait Five whenever they can about those people and their needs. We usually find that God's peace, next steps, and provision enter the situation.

> **Example:** A need may be the illness of someone. Just like in Luke 10:9 we will use our gifts and knowledge to heal, but mostly we will pray for healing. Then we use the opportunity to Wait Five by ourselves or with the ill person and any people around the person, bringing God into the situation directly.

Step 4: Tell people about Jesus.

Through Step 1 prayer the L-10-Ters have already started praying daily for God's blessing and salvation wherever they move and specifically on the people they connect with or care for. Through building relationships and meeting needs, L-10-Ters will have created an atmosphere of trust. Evangelism is primarily a process that starts with Step 1 and is not an event. L-10-Ters are already evangelists because they are drawing people around them closer to Jesus.

In Step 4 we are at a place where we can share our faith and tell our story with Jesus (our testimony). Next, we might feel that the Lord is encouraging us to share the gospel message of Jesus. By sharing Jesus, we encourage people to accept Him as their Savior; and they too become part of His story.

People with the gift of evangelism (Ephesians 4:11) might directly share the gospel one-on-one or in larger groups. We call them the 4% or "direct" evangelists. The other 96% who formerly (before L-10-T) were not evangelizing are now evangelists because they are drawing people around them closer to Jesus through Steps 1 to 3. In Step 4 they are trained to share their testimony and share the gospel message with people, so that they are ready to share when asked or when empowered by the Holy Spirit to take the initiative.

Take Five
A part of Step 4, we recognize that almost every believer has people in their family or among friends who do not yet believe in Jesus as Lord and Savior. Believers are likely concerned about the redemption of these people and may have shared the gospel with them repeatedly to no avail.

In L-10-T we encourage every L-10-Ter to select five of these well-known not-yet-believers and do the first three steps of L-10-T on them every day. When the time is right Step 4 is also done, one's testimony and the gospel are shared. This process should continue for at least a year or until they accept Jesus as Lord and Savior.

Waiting on God integrated into Step 4

The integration of Waiting on God into L-10-T Step 4 takes the process described to a new level as L-10-Ters practice Wait Five for the people with whom they will share their testimony and the gospel, including the people on their Take Five list. Andrew Murray speaks regularly about redemption and salvation in Waiting on God (especially Days 1, 2, 13, 17, 19, 25 and 27).

> **Example:** X is one of your Take Five (a child, parent, sibling, etc.). Every day you pray Step 1 for X, that the Lord will bless X to the fullest extent so that X may come to know Jesus as Lord and Savior. After your prayer for X (or for all five of your Take Five) you then Wait Five for X (or your Take Five) before the Lord. It brings you closer to the Lord's heart for X (or your Take Five).

Please note that the L-10-Ter's Take Five list does not normally include the targeted not-yet-believers identified in Step 2 to build a relationship with. This is a second list. Take Five people are usually well known to the L-10-Ter.

Also note that the believer is often not even the person who leads one of the Take Five to Christ. God is so good and He hear our cries on behalf of the lost!

How does L-10-T become a lifestyle?

The L-10-T course is an interesting course for believers to take (about 12 contact hours). But it does not avail much if the believer finishes the course, files away the course manual, and continues to live as before.

The L-10-T course is designed to assist every believer to live the L-10-T lifestyle daily everywhere they go; there is no retirement. An L-10-T lifestyle occurs as one simply lives this life of following Jesus without thinking about it in concrete steps or sub-steps. But, such a lifestyle must be developed over time as one repeats the steps daily. As people, we tend to resist change and forget to do new things. So, in the L-10-T training, we encourage everyone to have a buddy or L-10-T friend who can encourage you (and you, them) to remember and do the daily actions of following Jesus.

We also recommend and prefer that you meet regularly, every week, in a group of like-minded believers. Meetings can be in-home, over the phone, in a prayer group or virtual setting. They are designed to look back at the successes and failures of the past period. In-person meetings also allow you to lock hands in support and ask God together to assist with needs you discovered. Lastly, pray as you send each other out for the next period, just as Jesus did for the Luke 10 disciples.

Before you know it, L-10-T has become a lifestyle for you, your friends, and fellow L-10-T group members. In the L-10-T lifestyle, L-10-Ters touch many people (believers and not-yet-believers) by praying for God to touch them and waiting on God for them (Step 1). Many people (believers and not-yet-believers) are touched by L-10-Ters caring for their needs. Many not-yet-believers are drawn to Jesus as Savior by L-10-Ters doing Steps 2 and 4 and Taking Five.

L-10-T is especially powerful if an entire congregation sets L-10-T as their vision of a lifestyle following Jesus. **The result is transformation of the individual, current and new members of the congregation, the growth of the church and the planting of new churches near**

and far. The same can happen to the people in an organization in any sphere of society.

All people trained to do L-10-T are encouraged to train others to do L-10-T. **We call it Equip Five! Training others to do L-10-T is one of the best ways to learn to do L-10-T better.** There is also L-10-T Train-the-Trainer courses to equip L-10-Ters to train larger groups and to train other trainers. Furthermore, we have an L-10-T course to train L-10-Ters who want to train **children from ages 4 to 14 years to do L-10-T.**

L-10-T is truly a way to live as disciples who make disciples daily everywhere!

Waiting on God integrated into the L-10-T lifestyle
When individuals, buddies, L-10-T group members, and entire congregations or workplaces incorporate Waiting on God in all aspects of their doing L-10-T, **the result is awesome!** Suddenly all are waiting on God to act among them in all the ways as described in the 31 days of Waiting on God devotions.

"Our souls, wait only on God!"

Do not miss the joy of doing L-10-T with Waiting on God!

Believers who do L-10-T and share it among themselves experience great joy in the Lord! However, this result should not surprise us. After all, Luke 10:17 records that the 72 disciples Jesus sent out returned with great joy!

So, L-10-T now shows every believer how they can live a lifestyle of following Jesus and waiting on God, connecting with God and others, caring for people's needs, and sharing Jesus in a way that will draw people closer to God and their salvation. Truly, a "Praying-Connecting-Caring-and-Sharing Jesus" lifestyle.

If you want to know more about our integrated Waiting on God and L-10-T courses, please contact us at:

Colin Millar – colin@ignitingprayeraction.org

or

Willem Joubert – willemjoubert1@gmail.com

May the Lord bless you as you wait on him and do L-10-T!

Willem Joubert
July 2, 2022

This testimony of Waiting on God and Luke 10 Transformation is made by my dear friend and younger twin brother. He also translated Waiting on God into our first 2 African languages Kirundi and KiSwahili.

> Waiting on God is a mystery to knowing the mind and heart of God. I have been waiting on God from 1989. God has never disappointed me. Praying louder was my mentorship since my youth. However, keeping silent and hearing from God deepens my intimacy and friendship with God every day so much more than speaking to God. Yes, I do speak to God when I am interceding and praising and adoring Him. God has taught me to listen to Him rather than to speak to Him.

When you wait on God and live out the four steps of Luke 10 Transformation this is what happens:

1. It makes the heart grow with spiritual ingredients.

2. It is the best way to disciple true disciples of Jesus Christ who grow deeply in the word and passionately in missions.

3. It challenges the heart to proactively engage your own AND other lives in the great commission of making disciples of all nations.

4. It is dependable and unfailing.

5. People learn to hear God in a personal and life transforming way.

6. Disciples grow numerically and spiritually.

7. It fuels all church planting strategies because it engages every discipled heart.

8. It maximizes church mobilization for the entrusted mission of 2 Tim 2: 1-2. "So, my son, throw yourself into this work for Christ. Pass on what you heard from me—the whole congregation saying Amen!—to reliable leaders who are competent to teach others." ~ The Message.

9. It stirs up the inner spirit man connecting one to the utmost mind of God.

10. It grows strong, solid, reproducing church members committed to change the world and make disciples of all nations.

Dr. Bishop Evariste Harerimana
Burundi East Africa

Day 1

The God of Our Salvation

"Truly my soul silently waits for God;
from Him comes my salvation."—Psalm 62:1

If salvation indeed comes from God and is entirely His work (just as Creation was), it follows that our first and highest duty is to wait on God to complete that work as it pleases Him. Waiting becomes then the only way to experience our full salvation, and the only way to know the God of our salvation. Any difficulty we have in experiencing our full salvation is caused by this one thing: the defective knowledge and practice of waiting upon God. All that the church and its members need for the manifestation of the mighty power of God in the world is the return to our true place, that place where we truly belong—both in creation and in redemption—the place of *absolute and unceasing dependence upon God.* You may wonder what elements make up this most blessed and needful waiting upon God, and why this practice is so little cultivated? As we answer those questions, may we begin to feel how infinitely desirable it is that the church, that we ourselves, should at any price learn its blessed secret.

The deep need for this waiting on God lies equally in the nature of humankind and in the nature of God. God, as Creator, formed Adam to be a vessel from which His power and goodness would flow. Adam did not have in himself a fountain of life or strength or happiness; the ever-living One was each moment the Communicator to Adam of all that he needed. Adam's glory and blessedness were neither independent nor dependent upon himself, but dependent on the God of infinite riches and love. *Adam had the joy of receiving every moment out of the fullness of God.* This was his blessedness as an unfallen creature.

When Adam fell away from God, he became even more dependent on Him, not less. He had not the slightest hope of recovery from his state of sin or death, except in God through His power and mercy. It is God alone who began the work of redemption; it is God alone who continues that work each moment in each individual believer. Even in the regenerate person there is no power of goodness in oneself; the believer has and can have nothing that is not each moment received. Waiting on God is just as indispensable and must be just as continuous and unbroken as the breathing that maintains one's natural life.

It is only because Christians do not realize their relation to God of absolute poverty and helplessness, that they have no sense of their need of absolute and unceasing dependence, or of the unspeakable blessedness of continual waiting on God. But once a believer begins to sense it and consent to it, then the Holy Spirit gives each moment what God each moment works. Waiting on God becomes the believer's brightest hope and joy. Finally apprehending how God as Infinite Love delights to impart His own nature to His child, how God doesn't grow weary of each moment keeping charge of His child's life and strength, the believer wonders why he or she ever thought of God as anything other than as a God to be waited on all day long. God unceasingly giving and working; His child unceasingly waiting and receiving—this is the blessed life.

"Truly my soul silently waits for God; from Him comes my salvation." First, we wait on God for salvation. Then we learn that salvation merely brings us to God in order to teach us to wait on Him more. And finally we find what is better still, that waiting on God is itself the highest salvation. It is the ascribing to Him the glory of being All; it is the experiencing that He is All to us. May God teach us the blessedness of waiting on Him.

"My soul, wait only on God!"

Personal Reflection

Day 2

The Keynote of Life

"I have waited for your salvation, O Lord!"—Genesis 49:18

Jacob made this statement while prophesying about the future of his sons: "I have waited for your salvation, O Lord!" What did he mean by these words? They seem to indicate that his expectation—both for himself and for his sons—was from God alone. It was God's salvation he waited for; a salvation that God had promised and that God alone could accomplish. He acknowledged that he and his sons were under God's charge. The Everlasting God would demonstrate through their lives what His saving power could do. Jacob's words point forward to the wonderful story of redemption, which is not yet finished, and to the glorious future in eternity where it is leading. They suggest to us how there is no salvation but God's salvation, and how waiting on God for that—whether for our personal experience or for wider circles—is our first duty, our true blessedness.

Let us ponder the inconceivably glorious salvation God has provided for us in Christ and is even now working to perfect in us by His Spirit. Let us meditate until we somewhat realize that *every aspect of this great salvation, from moment to moment, must be the work of God himself.* God cannot part with His grace or goodness or strength as some external thing that He gives us, like raindrops from heaven. No, God can only give these things and we can only enjoy them as He provides them directly and unceasingly. And the only reason that God does not work His salvation more effectually and continuously is that we do not allow it. We hinder that work, either by our indifference or by our self-effort, so that God cannot do what He would. What is asked of us, in terms of surrender and obedience and desire and trust, is all comprised in this one word: *wait*, wait on God, wait for His salvation. It combines the deep sense of our entire helplessness to work what is divinely good with the perfect assurance that our God will work it all in His divine power.

Again, let us meditate on the glorious salvation God is working out in us, until we grasp the truths that it implies. Our heart is the scene of a divine operation more wonderful than the creation of the world. We contribute as little to the work of salvation as we did to creation, except as God works in us to will and to do. God only asks of us to yield, to consent, to wait upon Him, and He will do it all. Let us meditate and be still, until we see how wonderful and right and blessed it is that God alone does all. Then our soul will sink down in deep humility and say: "I have waited for your salvation, O Lord." And the deep blessed background of all our praying and working will be: "Truly my soul waits on God."

The application of this truth to wider circles—to those we labor among or intercede for, to the church of Christ around us or throughout the world—is not difficult. There can be no good but what God works. To wait on God, to be filled with faith that He is at work, and in that faith to pray for His mighty power to come down, is our only wisdom. Oh, may the eyes of our heart be opened to see God at work in ourselves and in others, and to see how blessed it is just to worship and to wait for His salvation!

Our private and public prayers are the chief expression of our relationship to God; it is in prayer that our waiting upon God must first be exercised. Our waiting begins by quieting the activities of nature and being still before God; it bows and seeks to see God in His universal and almighty operation, alone able and always ready to work all good; it yields itself to God in the assurance that He is working and will work in us; it maintains this place of humility and stillness and surrender until the Spirit infuses us with the faith that He will perfect His work. If we pray like this, our waiting will indeed become the strength and the joy of the soul. Life will become one deep blessed cry: "I have waited for your salvation, O Lord."

"My soul, wait only on God!"

Personal Reflection

Day 3

The True Place of the Creature

"These all wait for You, that you may give them their food in due season. What You give them they gather in; You open Your hand, they are filled with good."—Psalm 104:27-28

Psalm 104, in praise of the Creator, describes the beasts of the field, the birds of the heavens, and the animals of the forest; of man going out to his work until evening; and of the innumerable creatures of the great sea. Then it sums up the relationship of all creation to its Creator, its continuous and universal dependence upon Him with this profound declaration: *"These all wait for You!"* Just as it was God's work to create, so it is His work to maintain. Just as the creature could not create itself, so it cannot provide for itself. The whole of creation is ruled by one unalterable law: *It waits on God!*

This law expresses the one and only reason the creature was brought into existence. God brought creatures to life so that in them He might demonstrate His wisdom, power and goodness, His being each moment their life and happiness by pouring out to them, according to their capacity, the riches of His goodness and power. It is the very place and nature of God to be the continuous supplier of the creature's every need. Likewise, the very place and nature of the creature is only this—to wait upon God and receive from Him what He alone can give, what He delights to give.

If we hope to understand all that *waiting on God* means to the believer, to practice it and to experience its blessedness, then we must first see how very reasonable the call is to wait on God. We must understand how the duty is not an arbitrary command. We must see how it is made necessary by our sin and helplessness. It is simply and truly the restoration to our original destiny and our highest position, to our true place and glory as creatures blessedly dependent on our glorious God.

When our eyes are opened to this precious truth, all nature becomes a preacher, reminding us of the relationship that began in creation but now continues in grace. Psalm 104 teaches us to look upon all life in nature as continually maintained by God. Think of the young lions and the ravens as crying out to God, of the cattle and fish and every insect as waiting on Him to receive their food in due season, and you will see that it is the very nature and glory of God to be waited on. This understanding of how nature waits and that God provides gives new force to the call: "Wait only on God." This waiting on God is the very necessity of our being.

"These all wait for You that You may *give*." It is God who gives all: let this truth settle deeply into our hearts. Even before we fully understand all that it means to wait on God, and even before we have cultivated the habit, let the truth enter our souls: Waiting on God in unceasing and complete dependence on Him is the only true religion in heaven and on earth. Waiting is the one unalterable and comprehensive expression of true relationship to the ever-blessed One in whom we live.

Let us resolve that this will be the main characteristic of our life and worship, a continuous, humble, trustful waiting on God. We may rest assured that God who created us for Himself, in order to give Himself to us, will never disappoint us. By waiting on God may we find rest and joy and strength and the supply of every need.

"My soul, wait only on God"

Day 4

For Supplies

"The Lord upholds all who fall, and raises up all
who are bowed down. The eyes of all look expectantly
to You, and You give them their food in due season."
—Psalm 145:14-15

Psalm 104 is a psalm about creation, and the words *"These
all wait for You"* were used in reference to the animal world.
Here we have a psalm about the kingdom of God, and the
words *"The eyes of all look expectantly to You"* refer specifically to
God's saints, to all that fall and are bowed down. What the
universe and the animals do unconsciously, God's people are
meant to do intelligently and voluntarily. We are meant to be
the interpreter of nature. We are meant to prove that there is
nothing more noble or more blessed in the exercise of our free
will than to use it in waiting on God.

If an army has been sent out to march into enemy territory
and the report comes back that it is not advancing, the question
would be asked, "What is causing the delay?" The answer
very often might be, "Waiting for supplies." If the stores of
provisions or clothing or ammunition have not arrived, the
army dare not proceed. It is no different in the Christian life:
day by day, at every step, we need our supplies from above.
Our greatest need is to cultivate that spirit of dependence on
God and of confidence in Him, which refuses to go on without
an abundant supply of grace and strength.

You may ask how this is any different from what we do when we pray. The answer is that there may be *much praying with* but little waiting on God. In "praying with" we are often occupied with ourselves, with our own needs and with our own effort in the presentation of them. In waiting on God, our first thought is of the God on whom we wait. As we enter His presence, we feel the need just to be quiet, so that He as God can overshadow us. God longs to reveal Himself, to fill us with Himself. Waiting on God provides time for Him to come to us, in His own way and with divine power.

It is especially at the moment of prayer that we ought to cultivate this spirit of waiting. Before you begin to pray, bow quietly before God and seek to remember and realize who He is, how near He is, how certainly He can and will help. Just be still before Him. Allow the Holy Spirit to stir up in your soul the childlike attitude of absolute dependence and confident expectation. Wait upon God as the Living One, who notices you and who is just longing to work His salvation in you. Wait on God till you know you have met Him, then prayer will become so different.

And when you are praying, allow for intervals of silence, of reverent stillness of soul, in which you yield yourself to God. He may have something He wishes to teach you or to work in you. Waiting on God will become the most blessed part of prayer, and the answer to your prayer will be twice as precious because it is the fruit of close fellowship with the Living One. God has so ordained it, this harmony of His holy nature with ours, that waiting on Him should be the honor we give Him. Let us do so gladly and truthfully; He will reward us abundantly.

"The eyes of all look expectantly to You, and You give them their food in due season." Dear soul, God provides in nature for the creatures He has made; how much more will He provide in grace for those He has redeemed. Learn to say of every want, of every failure and of every spiritual lack: I have waited too little on God, otherwise He would have given me in due season all I needed.

"My soul, wait only on God!"

Personal Reflection

Day 5

For Instruction

"Show me Your ways, O Lord; teach me Your paths. Lead
me in Your truth and teach me, for You are the God of my
salvation; on You I wait all the day."—Psalm 25:4-5

I spoke of an army on the point of entering enemy territory,
answering the question as to the cause of delay, *"Waiting
for supplies."* The answer might also have been, *"Waiting for
instructions"* or *"Waiting for orders."* If the last dispatch had not
given the final orders of the commander-in-chief, the army
dared not move. This is also true in the Christian life; as great
as the need of *waiting for supplies* is that of *waiting for instructions.*

See how beautifully this comes out in Psalm 25. The writer
loved God's law above all else, and so he studied that law both
day and night. But he came to realize that even this devotion to
the law was not enough. For the right spiritual understanding
of the truth and for the right personal application of it to his
own peculiar circumstances, he needed direct divine teaching.

This particular psalm is a favorite one of many people,
perhaps because it expresses our deep longing for divine
guidance, along with the childlike confidence that guidance
would be given. Study the psalm until your heart is filled with
two thoughts—the absolute need and the absolute certainty of
divine guidance. Then notice how it is within this connection
that he speaks, *"On You I wait all the day."* Waiting for guidance,
waiting for instruction, all the day, is a very blessed part of
waiting upon God.

The Father in heaven is so interested in His children, and so longs to keep their every step within His will and His love, that He is willing to guide them entirely by His own hand. God knows that we are unable to do what is truly holy and heavenly without His help. God's demands actually become the promises of what He would do in watching over and leading us all day long. It is not only in times of difficulty and perplexity, but also in the common course of everyday life, that we may count on God to teach us *His* way and show us *His* path.

What do we need to do to receive this guidance? One thing: wait for instructions, wait on God. *"On You I wait all the day."* In our times of prayer, we will want to clearly express our sense of need, and our faith in God's promise to help. We will want to admit our ignorance of what God's way may be, and our need for divine light to shine within us. Only then will our way become like the sun, which "shines ever brighter unto the perfect day" (Proverbs 4:18). And we want to wait quietly before God in prayer, until a deep, restful assurance fills us. As the psalm also says, "The humble He teaches His way" (Psalm 25:9).

The special surrender to divine guidance in our times of prayer should cultivate the habit of looking upwards "all the day." Consider how simple it is to walk all the day in the light of the sun; it can become just as simple and delightful to a soul practiced in waiting on God, to walk all the day in the enjoyment of God's light and leading. What is needed to live such a life is this: a real knowledge of God as the only source of wisdom and goodness, and a faith in God as ever ready and longing to give us all that we could possibly need. If only we could see our God in His love, if only we could believe that He longs to be gracious, that He waits to be our life and to work His good in us, then this waiting on God would become our highest joy, the natural and spontaneous response of our hearts to His great love and glory.

O God, teach us, above everything else, the blessed lesson that all the day and every moment of it You surround us, doing Your work of love. Remind us that You only ask of us to wait on God. Help us to say, "ON YOU I WAIT ALL THE DAY."

"My soul, wait only on God!"

Personal Reflection

Day 6

For All Saints

"Let no one who waits on You be ashamed."—Psalm 25:3

As we quiet our hearts today, let us each forget about ourselves and consider instead that great company of God's saints throughout the world, all those who too are waiting on God. Then let us join in fervent prayer for each other, "Let no one who waits on You be ashamed."

Consider for a moment the multitude of waiting ones who need that prayer; think of those who are sick and weary and alone, whose prayers have not been answered and who are beginning to fear that their hope will be put to shame. Think too of the many servants of God, ministers or missionaries, teachers or workers, whose hopes for their work have been disappointed, and whose longing for divine power and blessing remains unsatisfied. Think too of the many who have embraced the promise of rest and perfect peace, of abiding light and fellowship, of strength and victory, yet who cannot find the path to that reality. In every case, the problem is they have not yet learned the secret of fully waiting on God. They just need, we all need, the assurance that waiting on God can never be in vain. So, let us remember all who are weary and in danger of fainting and unite in the cry, "Let no one who waits on You be ashamed!"

Only when this intercession for others who wait on God becomes part of our waiting on Him for ourselves, do we begin to bear one another's burdens and so fulfill the law of

Christ (Galatians 6:2). The elements of unselfishness and love are thereby introduced into our waiting on God, which is the path to the highest blessing and the fullest communion with God. God's love for His Son and for us are one and the same. Jesus prayed, "that the love with which You loved Me may be in them" (John 17:26). The love of the Father for Christ and Christ's love for us are the same: "As the Father loved Me, I also have loved you" (John 15:9). And then he asks us to extend that love to each other: "A new commandment I give to you, that you love one another; as I have loved you, that you also love one another" (John 13:34). The love of God and the love of Christ are inseparably linked with love for one another. What better way to prove and cultivate this love than by daily praying for each other? Christ did not seek to enjoy the Father's love alone; He shared it with His followers. All true seeking after God and His love will be inseparably linked with love and concern for other believers as expressed in our prayers for them.

"Let no one who waits on You be ashamed." Twice in this psalm David refers to himself as waiting on God; but then he considers *all* who wait on God. May it encourage all God's tried and weary ones to know that there are others praying for them. And may it motivate each of us in our waiting to forget about ourselves at times and to open our hearts, praying to the Father, "These all wait on You, and You give them their food in due season" (Psalm 104:27). May we all be inspired with new courage, for who doesn't at times feel weary and ready to faint? These words are to us a promise in a prayer, "Let no one who waits on You be ashamed!"

And may this be the cry of all who need help, who are discouraged: "Wait on the Lord; be of good courage, and He shall strengthen your heart; wait, I say, on the Lord!" (Psalm 27:14).

Dear Father, we humbly ask that no one who waits on You would be ashamed, not one. Some are weary, they feel they have waited a long time. Some are feeble, they don't know if they can hold on much longer. And some are so entangled in their work, they don't think they can spare the time to wait continually. Father, teach us all to wait. Teach us to forget ourselves and to pray for each other. Teach us to consider You, the God of all waiting ones. Father, let no one who waits on You be ashamed, for Jesus' sake. Amen.

"My soul, wait only on God!"

Personal Reflection

Day 7

A Plea in Prayer

"Let integrity and uprightness preserve me;
for I wait on You."—Psalm 25:21

For the third time in this psalm we find the word *wait*. As before in verse 5, "On You I wait all the day," so here too the psalmist appeals to God to remember that he is waiting on Him, looking for an answer. It is a great thing for a soul not only to wait on God, but to be filled with the awareness that its whole position is that of one who waits. In childlike confidence, it says, "Lord! You know, I wait on You." That confidence becomes a mighty plea in prayer, ever increasing the boldness of expectation to claim the promise, "They that wait on Me will not be ashamed!"

The connection between the pray-er (the one who prays) and the plea is of great importance in the spiritual life. If we draw near to God, it must be with a true heart. There must be perfect integrity, whole-heartedness, in our dealing with God. As Psalm 26 says, "Vindicate me, O Lord, for I have walked in my integrity." There must be perfect uprightness or single-heartedness before God. As it is written, His righteousness is for "the upright in heart" (Psalm 36:10). The soul must not harbor anything sinful or anything doubtful; indeed, to meet the holy God and receive His full blessing, it must be with a heart wholly surrendered to His will. The whole spirit that animates us in the waiting must be that of "integrity and uprightness." And we can be sure that God will "preserve" those who earnestly desire to meet with Him and who are looking to God to do His perfect work in them.

In our first attempt to live the life of full and continually waiting on God, we may discover how much we lack perfect integrity. If so, count this as just one of the many blessings that waiting is meant to work. We cannot seek close fellowship with God, nor attain the abiding consciousness of waiting on Him all the day, without complete honesty and entire surrender to all His will.

"For I wait on You." It is not only in connection with the prayer of today's text but with every prayer that this plea may be used. Using it often will bring us great blessing. Let us therefore study the words until we grasp their importance. It must be clear to us *what we are waiting for.* There may be very different things. It may be waiting for God in our times of prayer to take his place as God, and to work in us the sense of His holy presence and nearness. It may be a special petition, to which we are expecting an answer. It may be our whole inner life, in which we are seeking an outpouring of God's power. It may be the whole state of His church, or some part of His work, for which we are looking to Him. It is good to take account of exactly what things we are waiting for, and as we say definitely of each of them, "On You do I wait," we shall be emboldened to claim the answer, "*For* I wait on You!"

It must also be clear to us, *on whom we are waiting.* Not an idol, a god made in the image of our own conceptions. No, but the living God, such as He really is in His great glory, His infinite holiness, power, wisdom and goodness, in His love and nearness. It is the presence of a beloved or a dreaded master that awakens the whole attention of the servant who waits on him. It is *the presence of God, as He makes Himself known in Christ by the Holy Spirit,* and keeps the soul under its covering and shadow, that will awaken and strengthen the true waiting spirit. Let us be still and wait and worship till we know how near He is, and then say, "On You do I wait."

Finally, let it be clear that we are *waiting*. Let that become so much our consciousness that we say spontaneously, "On You do *I wait* all the day; *I wait* on You." This will indeed imply sacrifice and separation, a soul entirely surrendered to God as its all, its only joy. This waiting on God has hardly yet been acknowledged as the only true Christianity. And yet, if it be true that God alone is goodness and joy and love; if it be true that our highest blessedness is in having as much of God as we can; if it be true that Christ has redeemed us wholly for God and made a life of continual abiding in His presence possible, nothing less ought to satisfy our soul than to be ever breathing this blessed atmosphere, "I wait on You."

"My soul, wait only on God!"

Personal Reflection

Day 8

Strong and of Good Courage

"Wait on the Lord; be of good courage,
and He shall strengthen your heart; wait,
I say, on the Lord!"—Psalm 27:14

The psalmist further stated, "I would have lost heart, unless I had believed that I would see the goodness of the Lord in the land of the living" (Psalm 27:13). If it had not been for his faith in God, he would have lost heart. But in the confident assurance in God that faith gives, he urges himself and us to remember one thing above all, to wait on God. "Wait on the Lord; be of good courage." One of the greatest needs, one of the deepest secrets of blessing, is a quiet, confident persuasion that our waiting is not in vain. We need the courage to believe that God will hear and help; we are waiting on a God who could never disappoint His people

Be strong and of good courage. These words are typically spoken in connection with some great and difficult enterprise, as in the prospect of combat with powerful enemies, or in the utter insufficiency of human strength. Is waiting on God a work so difficult that such words are needed for it too? "Be of good courage, and He shall strengthen your heart." Yes, indeed. The deliverance for which we often wait is from enemies in whose presence we are impotent. The blessings for which we plead are spiritual and unseen, things humanly impossible; they are heavenly, supernatural, divine realities. We are so little accustomed to real fellowship with God that so often the God on whom we wait *appears* to hide Himself. We who wait may begin to fear that we don't know quite how to wait, or that our faith is too weak, or that our desire is not as earnest as it should be, or that our surrender is not complete. We may indeed grow faint of heart. Then in the midst of all our fears and doubts we hear that blessed word: "Wait on the Lord; be of good courage, and He shall strengthen your heart; wait, I say, on the Lord!" Nothing in heaven or earth or hell should prevent us from waiting on God in full assurance that our faith is not in vain.

The primary lesson our text teaches us is this: that when we set ourselves to wait on God, we need to resolve beforehand that we will wait with the most confident expectation of God's meeting and blessing us. We need to make up our minds about this, we can be assured that waiting on God will bring us untold and unexpected blessing. We are so accustomed to judging God's work in us by *what we feel*, that when we begin the practice of waiting on Him, we will most likely be discouraged because we do not sense any special blessing from it. Above everything, when you wait on God, do so in the spirit of great hopefulness. It is God in His glory, in His power and in His love longing to bless you that you are waiting on.

If you are afraid of deceiving yourself with false hope, because you do not see or feel anything in your present state to warrant such special expectations, my answer is, God is the warrant for your expectation of great things. Oh, do learn the lesson. Do not wait on yourself to see what you feel and what changes come to you. WAIT ON GOD—first to know WHO HE IS, and then, what He will do. The whole duty and blessing of waiting on God is rooted in this, that He is such a blessed being, overflowing with goodness and power and life and joy, that we as wretched beings cannot for any length of time have contact with Him, without that life and power secretly and silently beginning to enter into us and blessing us. God is love! That is the all-sufficient warrant for your expectation. Love seeks out its own: God's love is simply His *delight to impart Himself and His blessings* to His children. Come, no matter how weak you feel, and just wait in His presence. As a feeble, sickly invalid is brought out into the sunshine to soak in its warmth, bring all that is dark and cold in you *into the sunshine of God's omnipotent love.* Sit and wait there, with the one thought: *Here I am, in the sunshine of His love.* As the sun does its work in the weak one who seeks its rays, *God will do His work in you.* Oh, do trust Him fully. "Wait on the Lord; be of good courage, and He shall strengthen your heart; wait, I say, on the Lord!"

"My soul, wait only on God!"

Personal Reflection

Day 9

With the Heart

"Be strong, and let your heart take courage,
all you who wait for the Lord."—Psalm 31:24 (ESV)

The wording of this verse is nearly the same as the one in our last meditation. But I have chosen it to press home a much-needed lesson for all who desire to learn truly and fully what waiting on God means. The lesson is this: It is *with the heart* that we must wait for God. "Let *your heart* take courage." All our waiting depends on the state of the heart. As our heart is, so are we before God. We can advance no further into the holy place of God's presence to wait on Him there, than our heart is prepared for it by the Holy Spirit. The message is, "Let *your heart* take courage, all you that wait on the Lord."

This truth appears so simple that some may ask, but don't we all admit this? Why insist on it especially? I do so because too many Christians do not recognize the great difference between the religion of the mind and the religion of the heart; and the former is far more diligently cultivated than the latter. They don't know how infinitely greater the heart is than the mind. This is a primary cause of the feebleness of our Christian life, and only as this is understood will our waiting on God bring its full blessing.

Proverbs 3:5 may help to clarify this idea. Speaking of living in the fear and favor of God, it says, "Trust in the Lord with all your heart, and lean not on your own understanding."

In all areas of faith we must use these two powers, the mind and the heart. The mind gathers knowledge from God's Word and prepares the food by which the inner life of the heart is nourished. But herein lies a terrible danger, that of leaning on our own understanding and trusting in our apprehension of divine things. People imagine that if they are occupied with the truth, then the spiritual life will as a matter of course be strengthened. But this is not the case. The mind may be filled with conceptions and images of divine things, but it cannot reach the real life of the soul. Hence the command, "Trust in the Lord with *all your heart*, and lean not on your own understanding." It is with the heart that a person believes and comes into contact with God. It is in the heart where the Holy Spirit comes to live, to be the presence and the power of God working in us. In every aspect of our faith, it is the heart that must trust and love and worship and obey. My mind is utterly impotent in creating or maintaining the spiritual life within me: the heart must wait on God to do that work in me.

Compare this to the physical life. My mind may tell me what to eat and drink, and I may even understand how that food nourishes me. But understanding those things in my mind does nothing to my body; the body has special organs for the purpose of eating and digesting food. Just so, the mind may tell me what God's Word says, but that doesn't feed the soul with the bread of life. This the heart alone can do by faith and trust in God. Likewise, a man may be studying the effects of food or sleep on the body; but when he needs to eat or sleep, he sets aside his books and uses the power of eating or sleeping. Just so, when the believer has studied or heard God's Word, there comes the time to cease from those thoughts, to put no trust in them, and to simply open up one's heart before God and seek living fellowship with Him.

This is the blessed state of waiting on God: that I confess the impotence of all my thoughts and efforts, and bow in holy silence before Him, trusting Him to renew and strengthen my heart. This is the lesson of our text, "Let *your heart* take courage, all you who wait on the Lord." Remember the difference between knowing with the mind and believing with the heart. Beware of the temptation of leaning on your own understanding, with its clear strong thoughts. They only help you to know what it is the heart needs from God: thoughts are mere images and shadows. "Let *your heart* take courage, all you who wait on the Lord." Present your heart to Him as that wonderful part of your spiritual nature in which God reveals Himself, and by which you can know Him. Cultivate the greatest confidence that, though you cannot see into your heart, God is working there by the Holy Spirit. Let the heart wait at times in perfect silence and quiet; in its hidden depths God will work. Be sure of this, and just wait on Him.

No knowledge of the air or the food around me can nourish me, except as they enter into my inward life. And no knowledge of the truths of God can benefit me, except as the Holy Spirit enters my inmost being and dwells within me. It is with the heart I must wait on God; it is in the heart where I must receive God; it is to the heart God gives the Spirit and every spiritual blessing in Christ. Place your whole heart, with its secret workings, into God's hands continually. He wants your heart and takes it so that He might take up residence in it. "Be strong, and let *your heart* take courage, all you who wait on the Lord."

"My soul, wait only on God!"

Personal Reflection

60

Day 10

In Humble Fear and Hope

"Behold, the eye of the Lord is on those who fear
Him, on those who hope in His mercy, to deliver their
soul from death, and to keep them alive in famine.
Our soul waits for the Lord; He is our help and our
shield. For our heart shall rejoice in Him, because we
have trusted in His holy name. Let Your mercy,
O Lord, be upon us, just as we hope in You."
—Psalm 33:18-22

God's eye is upon His people; their eye is upon Him. When
we wait on God, our eye looks up to Him and meets His
eye looking down on us. This is the blessedness of waiting
on God, that it takes our eyes and thoughts off ourselves, off
our needs and desires, and focuses our eyes on our God. We
worship Him in His glory and love, with His all-seeing eye
watching over us, that He may supply our every need. Let us
consider this wonderful meeting between God and His people;
note especially what is being taught here about *those on whom
God's eye rests,* and about *Him on whom our eye rests.*

"The eye of the Lord is on those who fear Him, on those
who hope in His mercy." Fear and hope are generally thought to
be in conflict with each other; but in the presence of God they
are found side by side in perfect and beautiful harmony. This
is because in God all apparent contradictions are reconciled.
Righteousness and peace, judgment and mercy, holiness and
love, infinite power and infinite gentleness, a majesty that is
exalted above the heavens and a condescension that bows to the

ground—these meet and kiss each other. There is a tormented kind of fear that is cast out entirely by perfect love (1 John 4:18). But there is another kind of fear that endures forever in heaven. John witnessed the song of Moses and the Lamb being sung in heaven: "Who shall not fear You, O Lord, and glorify Your name?" (Revelation 15:4). "Then a voice came from the throne, saying, "Praise our God, all you His servants and those who fear Him, both small and great!" (Revelation 19:5).

In our waiting let us always "fear this glorious and awesome name, THE LORD YOUR GOD" (Deuteronomy 28:58). The deeper we bow before God in holy fear and adoring awe, in deep reverence and humble self-abasement, even as the angels veil their faces before the throne, the more will His holiness rest on us and the more will our souls be ready for God to reveal Himself. The deeper we delve into the truth "that no flesh should glory in His presence" (1 Corinthians 1:29), the more will we be allowed to see His glory. "The eye of the Lord is on those who fear Him, on those who hope in His mercy." The true fear of God will not diminish hope, rather it will stimulate and strengthen it. The lower we bow, the deeper we feel we have nothing to hope in but His mercy. The lower we bow, the nearer God will come and the bolder our hearts will be made to trust Him. Let every exercise of waiting, let our whole habit of waiting on God, be permeated with abounding hope, a hope as bright and boundless as God's mercy. The fatherly kindness of God is such that, in whatever state we come to Him, we may confidently hope in His mercy.

Such are God's waiting ones. And now, let us think about the God on whom we wait. "The eye of the Lord is on those who fear Him, on those who hope in His mercy; to deliver their soul from death, and to keep them alive in famine." The promise is not to prevent the danger of death and famine— this is often needed to stir the waiting on Him—but to deliver and to keep alive. The dangers are often very real and dark; the situation, whether in the temporal or spiritual life, may appear to be utterly hopeless. Yet there is always hope: *God's eye is on them.* That eye sees the danger, and sees in tender love His trembling waiting child; that eye also sees the moment when the heart is ripe for the blessing, and sees the way in which it is to come. Oh, let us fear this living, mighty God and hope in His mercy. And let us humbly but boldly say, "Our soul waits for the Lord; He is our help and our shield. Let Your mercy, O Lord, be upon us, just as we wait for You."

Oh, the blessedness of waiting on such a God—a very present help in every time of trouble, a shield and defense against every danger! Children of God, learn to sink down in complete helplessness and impotence and to wait in stillness for the salvation of God. During the utmost spiritual famine or when death seems near, oh, wait on God! He does deliver, He does keep alive. Say it not only to oneself, but say it to each other, just as the psalmist speaks not only of himself but of God's people: "*Our* soul waits for the Lord. He is *our* help and *our* shield." Strengthen and encourage each other in the holy exercise of waiting, that each may say not only of oneself, but also of God's people, "*We* have waited for Him; *we* will be glad and rejoice in His salvation."

"My soul, wait only on God!"

Personal Reflection

Day 11

Waiting Patiently

"Rest in the Lord, and wait patiently for Him;
but those who wait on the Lord, they shall
inherit the earth." —Psalm 37:7, 9

Consider also these verses: "By your patience possess your souls" (Luke 21:19). "For you have need of endurance" (Hebrews 10:36). "But let patience have its perfect work, that you may be perfect and complete, lacking nothing" (James 1:4). Such words of the Holy Spirit show us how important patient endurance is in the Christian life and character. And there is no better place for cultivating or displaying patience than in waiting on God. There we discover how impatient we are, and what our impatience indicates. We confess at times to being impatient with others and circumstances that hinder us, or with ourselves and our slow progress in the Christian life. But when we sincerely begin to wait on God, we find that it is with God that we are truly impatient, because He does not immediately do our bidding. It is in waiting on God that our eyes are opened to see His wise and sovereign will, and to understand that the sooner and more completely we yield to that will, the more surely His blessing can come to us.

"So then it is not of him who wills, nor of him who runs, but of God who shows mercy" (Romans 9:16). We have as little power to strengthen our spiritual life, as we had to originate it. We "were born not of the will of the flesh, nor of the will of man, but of the will of God" (John 1:13). Even so, our willing and running, our desire and effort, accomplish nothing, for all is done by God who has mercy on us. All the exercises of the spiritual life, our reading and praying, our willing and doing, have merit. But they can do no more than point the way and prepare us in humility to depend alone on God, and to wait patiently for His perfect timing. The waiting serves to teach us absolute dependence on God's mighty working, and to make us place ourselves at His disposal in perfect patience. Those who wait on the Lord shall inherit the earth. The heirs must wait; they can afford to wait.

"Rest in the Lord, and wait patiently for Him." Another translation for "rest" is "be silent." "Be silent before the Lord," or "Be still before the Lord." It is resting in the Lord, in His will and promise and faithfulness and love, that makes patience easy. And the resting in the Lord is nothing but being silent before Him, still before Him. Our thoughts and wishes, our fears and hopes are hushed in that great peace of God which passes all understanding. That peace calms the heart and quiets the mind when we are anxious for anything, because we have made our request known to God. The rest, the silence, the stillness and the patient waiting —all find their strength and joy in God Himself.

It will be revealed to the waiting soul just how very reasonable and blessed patience is. Our patience will be seen as the counterpart of God's patience. He longs far more to bless us than we desire the blessing. But as "the farmer waits for the precious fruit of the earth, waiting patiently for it until it receives the early and latter rain," so God accommodates our slowness and waits along with us (James 5:7). Let us remember this and wait patiently. This word is true of each promise and every answer to prayer: "I the Lord will hasten it *in its time*" (Isaiah 60:22). "Rest in the Lord, and wait patiently for Him." Yes, for HIM. Seek not only the help, the gift, the supply; seek HIM; wait FOR HIM. Give God glory by resting in Him, by trusting Him fully, by waiting patiently for Him. This patience honors Him greatly; it seats Him as God on the throne to do His work; it yields oneself wholly into His hands. It lets God *be God*. If you are waiting for some special request, wait patiently. If you are seeking to know and have more of God, wait patiently. Whether it be in the shorter specific periods of waiting, or as the continuous habit of the soul; rest in the Lord, be still before the Lord, and wait patiently. "Those who wait on the Lord shall inherit the earth."

"My soul, wait only on God!"

Personal Reflection

Day 12

Keeping His Ways

"Wait on the Lord, and keep His way, and He shall
exalt you to inherit the land."—Psalm 37:34

If we were longing to meet someone in particular, we would
inquire about the places and the ways where that person may
be found. When waiting on God, we need to be careful that
we keep to His ways; out of them we can never expect to find
Him. As the prophet said: "You meet him who rejoices and
does righteousness, who remembers You in Your ways" (Isaiah
64:5). We may be sure that God is never and nowhere to be
found but in His ways. And it is there, by the soul who seeks
and patiently waits, that He most surely will be found. "Wait
on the Lord, and keep His way, and He shall exalt you."

Notice how close the connection is between the two parts
of this injunction: "Wait on the Lord," which involves worship
and disposition; "and keep His way," which involves walk and
work. The outer life must be in harmony with the inner life;
the inner must provide the inspiration and the strength for the
outer. God makes known His ways in His word for our conduct
and invites our confidence for His grace and help in our heart.
If we do not keep His ways, our waiting on Him can bring no
blessing. The full surrender in obedience to all His will is the
secret of full access to all the blessings of His fellowship.

These truths are spelled out in Psalm 37, which speaks of
the evildoer who prospers in his way, yet calls on the believer
not to fret. We may observe people who seem prosperous and

happy but who have forsaken God's ways; in comparison, we may see ourselves as struggling or suffering. We need to stop right there. We are in danger of first fretting at this disparity and then forsaking God's way to seek our prosperity in the path of the ungodly. We must do as the psalm says: "Rest in the Lord, and wait patiently for Him; do not fret because of him who prospers in his way, because of the man who brings wicked schemes to pass. Cease from anger, and forsake wrath.... Depart from evil and do good; for the Lord loves justice, and does not forsake His saints; they are preserved forever....The law of his God is in his heart; none of his steps shall slide." And then follows for the third time in the psalm, *"Wait on the Lord, and keep His way."* Do what God asks you to do; and God will do more than you can ask Him to do.

Do not give way to the fear: I cannot keep His ways. This will rob you of your confidence. It is true you lack the strength yet to keep all His ways. But take care to keep those for which you have received strength already. Surrender yourself willingly and trustingly to keep all God's ways, in the strength that will come in waiting on Him. Present your whole being to God without reservation and without doubt. He will prove Himself God to you, and work in you that which is pleasing in His sight through Jesus Christ. Keep His ways, as you know them in the Word. Keep His ways, as nature teaches them. Keep His ways, in always doing what appears right. Keep His ways, as the Holy Spirit suggests. If you are not willing to walk in His path, don't even think about waiting on God. However weak you may feel, only be willing; and God who has worked in you to will, will also give you the power to do.

"Wait on the Lord, and keep His way." It may be that our awareness of some shortcoming and sin makes our text look more like a hindrance than a help in waiting on God. Let it not be so. Has it not been said more than once, the very starting point of this waiting is utter and absolute impotence? Why then not come with everything evil you feel in yourself, every memory of unwillingness, unwatchfulness, unfaithfulness, anything that causes self-condemnation? Put your trust in God's omnipotence and find in waiting on God your deliverance. Your past failure has been due to only one thing: you tried to conquer and obey in your own strength. Come and bow before God until you learn that He alone is good, and He alone can work any good thing. Realize that in you, in all that nature can do, there is no true power. Be content to receive from God each moment the inner working of His mighty grace and life. And then waiting on God will become the renewal of your strength to run in His ways and not be weary, to walk in His paths and never faint (Isaiah 40:31). The verse, "Wait on the Lord, and keep His way" will be command and promise in one.

"My soul, wait only on God!"

Personal Reflection

Day 13

For More Than We Know

"And now, Lord, what do I wait for? My hope is in You. Deliver me from all my transgressions."—Psalm 39:7-8

There may be times when we must admit that we do not really know what we are waiting for. At other times we may think we know, but even then it would be better for us to realize that we do not really know what is best. God is able to do for us "exceedingly abundantly above all that we ask or think" (Ephesians 3:20). We are in danger of limiting Him when we confine our desires and prayers to our own thoughts. It is a great thing at times to say, as our text reads: "And now, Lord, what do I wait for?" We scarcely know; we can only say, "My hope is in You."

We see this limiting of God in the case of Israel. When Moses promised them meat in the wilderness, they doubted, saying, "Can God prepare a table in the wilderness? Behold, He struck the rock, so that the waters gushed out, and the streams overflowed. Can He give bread also? Can He provide meat for His people?" (Psalm 78:19-20). If they had been asked whether God could provide streams in the desert, they would have answered, "Yes." God had done it once; He could do it again. But when the thought came of God doing something new, they limited Him; their present expectation could not rise beyond their past experience or above their own imagination of what was possible. Even so, we may be limiting God by our conceptions of what He has promised or is able to do. Let us beware of limiting the Holy One of Israel in our prayers. Let us believe that every promise of God that we claim has divine meaning, infinitely beyond our understanding. Let us believe that He can fulfill his promises with a power and an abundance of grace beyond our wildest imagination. And let us therefore cultivate the habit of waiting on God, not only for what we think we need, but for all He is ready to do for us in his power and grace.

In every true prayer there are two hearts at work. The one is your heart, with its small, dark human thoughts of what you need and of what God can do. The other is God's great heart, with its infinite possibilities and divine purposes of blessing. What do you think? To which of these two hearts should you give the larger place in prayer? Undoubtedly, to the heart of God: everything depends on knowing and being occupied with that. But how little this is done. This is what waiting on God is meant to teach you. As you think of God's wonderful love and redemption, consider what these words must mean to Him. Confess how little you understand what God is willing to do for you, and say each time you pray: "And now, what do I wait for?" My heart cannot say. God's heart knows and waits to give. "My hope is in You." Wait on God to do for you more than you can ask or think.

Apply this practice to the prayer that follows: "Deliver me from all my transgressions." You may have prayed to be delivered from temper or pride or selfishness, seemingly in vain. If so, may it be that you had your own ideas about the way or to the extent God would do it? You may not have waited on God to do for you what you could not possibly conceive according to the riches of His glory. Learn to worship God as the God who does wonders, who wishes to prove in you that He can do something supernatural and divine. Bow before Him, wait upon Him, until your soul realizes that it is in the hands of a divine and almighty worker. Consent not to know what and how He will work; expect it to be something altogether godlike, something you must wait for in deep humility and receive only by divine power. Let the words, "And now, Lord, what do I wait for? My hope is in You," reflect the spirit behind every longing and every prayer. He will in His time do His good work.

Dear soul, in waiting on God you may often grow weary, because you don't know what to expect. I urge you, be of good courage. This admission of ignorance is often one of the best steps you can take. He is teaching you to leave all in His hands and to wait on Him alone. Wait on the Lord! Be strong and let your heart be encouraged. Yes, wait on the Lord!

"My soul, wait only on God!"

Personal Reflection

Day 14

The Way to the New Song

"I waited patiently for the Lord, and He inclined to me and heard my cry....He has put a new song in my mouth, even praise to our God."—Psalm 40:1-3

True patience is so foreign to our self-confident nature, yet it is so indispensable in our waiting on God. It is such an essential element of true faith, that we will once again meditate on what the word can teach us.

The word *patience* is derived from the Latin word for *suffering*. It suggests the state of being under the constraint of some power from which we would like to be free. At first, we may submit against our will; experience teaches us that when it is useless to resist, patient endurance is our wisest course. In waiting on God, it is of infinite consequence that we submit, not only because we are compelled to, but because we lovingly and joyfully consent to remain in the hands of our blessed Father. Patience then becomes our highest blessedness and our highest grace. Patience honors God and gives Him time to work in us. It is the highest expression of our faith in His goodness and faithfulness. It brings the soul perfect rest in the assurance that God is carrying on His work. It is the mark of our agreement that God may deal with us in such a way and time as He thinks best. True patience is the losing of our will in His perfect will.

Such patience is needed to reap the full benefits of waiting on God. And it is the fruit of our first lessons in the school of waiting. To many it will seem strange just how difficult it is truly to wait on God. The great stillness of soul that sinks into its own helplessness and waits for God to reveal Himself; the deep humility that hesitates to do anything in its own will or own strength except as God works to will and to do; the meekness that is content to be and to know nothing except as God gives His light; the entire resignation of the will that only wants to be a vessel through which the Holy Spirit can move and flow: all these elements of perfect patience do not appear at once. But they will come into maturity as the soul maintains its position and continues to say: "Truly my soul silently waits for God; from Him comes my salvation: He only is my rock and my salvation" (Psalm 62:1).

Have you ever noticed that patience is a grace for which special help is given? Paul wrote that the saint is *"strengthened with all might, according to His glorious power."* And for what? *"For all patience and longsuffering with joy"* (Colossians 1:11). Yes, we need to be strengthened with all God's might, with the full measure of His glorious power, if we are to wait on God with perfect patience. As God reveals Himself to us as our life and strength, we are enabled with perfect patience to leave all in His hands. If you are inclined to despair because you don't have such patience, take heart; it is during the course of our feeble and imperfect waiting that God by His hidden power strengthens us and nurtures in us the patience of the saints, the patience of Christ Himself.

Listen to the voice of one in deep distress: "I waited patiently for the Lord, and He inclined to me, and heard my cry." Hear what he passed through: "He also brought me up out of a horrible pit, out of the miry clay. He has set my feet upon a rock and established my steps. He has put a new song in my mouth—praise to our God" (Psalm 40:2-3). Patient waiting on God brings a rich reward; the deliverance is sure; God Himself will put a new song into your mouth. Oh, believer, don't grow impatient! Whether it be in the exercise of prayer and worship that you find it difficult to wait, or in the delayed answer to specific requests, or in your heart's desire for a deeper revelation of God Himself—do not fear, but rest in the Lord and wait patiently for Him. And whenever you feel that patience is not your gift, remind yourself that it *is God's gift,* and then claim this prayer: "Now may the Lord direct your hearts into the love of God and into the patience of Christ" (2 Thessalonians 3:5). The Lord himself will guide you into the patience with which you are to wait on Him.

"My soul, wait only on God!"

Personal Reflection

Day 15

For His Counsel

"They soon forgot His works: they did not wait for His counsel:
...But they rebelled in their counsel."—Psalm 106:13, 43

This text describes the sin of God's people in the wilderness. God had wonderfully redeemed them from Egypt, and was prepared just as wonderfully to supply their every need. But, when the time of need came, "they did not wait for His counsel." They had not come to think of Almighty God as their leader and provider; so they did not think to ask what His plans might be. They simply followed what they thought best, and so rebelled against God in their unbelief: "They did not wait for His counsel."

This has been the sin of God's people through the ages. In conquering the land of Canaan during the days of Joshua, the only three failures they experienced were due to this one sin. In going up against Ai, in making a covenant with the Gibeonites, in settling down before pressing on to possess the whole land, they did not wait for His counsel. Even the mature believer is in danger of this most subtle of temptations—reading God's word and thinking one's own thoughts of them without waiting for His counsel. Let us heed the warning and learn from Israel's mistake. And let us especially regard it not only as a danger to the individual believer, but also as a danger against which God's people, in their collective capacity, need to be on guard.

Our whole relation to God is rooted in this, that His will is to be done on earth as it is in heaven. He has promised to make known His will to us by His Spirit, the Guide into all truth. And our position is to be that of waiting for His counsel, as the only guide of our thoughts and actions. In our church worship, in our prayer meetings, in our conventions, in our gatherings as managers or directors or committees or helpers in any area of God's work, our first objective must be to ascertain the mind of God. God always works according to the counsel of His will; so the more that counsel of His will is sought and found and honored, the more surely and mightily will God do His work in us and through us.

The great danger in all church assemblies is that we trust in our Bible knowledge, in our past experience of God's leading, in our sound creed, or in our honest wish to do God's will. And we fail to realize that our every step needs and can have heavenly guidance. There may be elements of God's will, applications of God's word, experiences of the close presence and leading of God, manifestations of the power of His Spirit, of which we know nothing yet. God may be willing, no, God is willing to reveal these to those who are intent on allowing God to have His way entirely, and who are willing to wait patiently for Him to make it known. When we come together, praising God for all He has done and taught and given, we may at the same time be limiting Him by not expecting greater things. It was after God had provided water out of the rock that the Israelites did not trust Him for bread. It was after God had given Jericho into his hands that Joshua thought victory over Ai was a sure thing; he thought he knew what God would do and so didn't wait for further counsel. And so, while we may think that we trust the power of God and know what to expect, we may actually be hindering the work of God by not taking the time and cultivating the habit of *waiting for His counsel.*

A minister has no more solemn duty than teaching people to wait on God. Why was it that in the house of Cornelius, "while Peter was still speaking these words, the Holy Spirit fell upon all those who heard the word" (Acts 10:44)? Perhaps it was because earlier they had stated, "We are all present before God, to hear all the things commanded you by God" (Acts 10:33). We may come together either to give or to listen to the most earnest exposition of God's truth and reap little spiritual profit because there has not first occurred the waiting for God's counsel. In all our gatherings, we need to rely on the Holy Spirit as the Guide and Teacher of God's saints and learn to wait for His leading into the things that God has prepared, the things our minds cannot conceive.

More stillness of soul to realize God's presence; more confession of ignorance of what God's great plans may be; more faith in the certainty that God can do greater things; more longing that God will be revealed in new glory—these must characterize the assembly of God's saints if they would avoid the reproach: "They did not wait for His counsel."

"My soul, wait only on God!"

Personal Reflection

Day 16

For His Light in the Heart

"I wait for the Lord, my soul waits, and in His word I do hope. My soul waits for the Lord more than those who watch for the morning, yes, more than those who watch for the morning."—Psalm 130:5-6

With what intense longing the morning light is often waited for! By the mariners in a shipwrecked vessel; by an overnight traveler in a dangerous area; by an army that finds itself surrounded by an enemy. The morning light will show what the chance for survival may be. The morning may bring rescue and safety. The psalmist who sat in spiritual darkness longed for the light of God's countenance, even more than watchmen long for the morning. He wrote, "More than those who watch for the morning, my soul waits for the Lord." Can we say that too? Our waiting on God can have no higher aim than simply to experience His light shining on us, and in us, and through us, all day long.

God is light. God is a sun. Paul says: "God...has shone in our hearts to give the light." What light? "The light of the knowledge of the glory of God in the face of Jesus Christ" (2 Corinthians 4:6). Just as the sun shines its beautiful, life-giving light upon our earth, so God shines into our hearts the light of His glory, the light of His love, as reflected in Christ His Son. Our heart was created for that light to fill and brighten it all day long. And this is possible because God is our sun, as it is written, "Your sun shall no longer go down" (Isaiah 60:20). God's love shines on us without ceasing.

But can we truly enjoy the light of God all day long? We can! How can we? Let nature give us the answer. Imagine a planting of beautiful trees and flowers surrounded by an expanse of green grass: what must they do to keep the sun shining on them? Nothing at all! They simply bask in the sunshine when it comes. The sun is millions of miles away, but over all that distance it sends its own light and joy; and the tiniest flower that lifts its little head upwards is met by the same exuberance of light and blessing as floods the widest landscape. We don't worry about the light we need for our day's work; the sun comes up and provides and shines its light around us all day long. We simply count on it and receive it and enjoy it.

The only difference between nature and grace is this, that what the trees and the flowers do unconsciously, as they drink in the blessing of the sunlight, we do with voluntary and loving acceptance. Through simple faith in God's word and love, we open up our eyes and open up our hearts to receive and enjoy the unspeakable glory of His grace. And even as the trees, day by day and month by month, stand and grow in their beauty and fruitfulness, just welcoming whatever light the sun may give, so it is the highest exercise of the Christian life just to abide in the light of God, allowing Him to fill us with the life and the brightness it brings.

But is it truly possible to rejoice in God's light as naturally and heartily as I recognize and rejoice in the beauty of a bright sunny morning? Yes, it is possible. From my breakfast table I look out on a beautiful valley, with trees and vineyards and mountains. In the spring and autumn months the morning light is exquisite, and almost involuntarily we say, "How beautiful!" So, I ask, is it only the light of the sun that can bring such continual beauty and joy? Has God not provided for His light to be just as much an unending source of joy and gladness? He has indeed, if the soul will just be still and wait on Him, ONLY LET GOD SHINE.

Dear soul, learn to wait on the Lord, more than watchers wait for the morning. All within you may seem very dark; but isn't that the best reason to wait for the light of God? The first dawning of light may be just enough to uncover the darkness, and to humble you on account of sin. Can you trust the light to expel the darkness? Do believe it will. Just bow, even now, in stillness before God, and *wait on Him* to shine on you. Say, in humble faith, God is light, infinitely brighter and more beautiful than that of the sun. God is light: the Father, the eternal, inaccessible and incomprehensible light; the Son, the light concentrated, embodied and manifested; the Spirit, the light entering, dwelling and shining in our hearts. God is light and is here shining on your heart.

Have you been so occupied with the flickers of your thoughts and efforts, that you have never opened the shutters to let His light shine in? Has unbelief kept it out? Bow in faith: God's light is shining into your heart. Claim the words of Paul for yourself, "God has shone on my heart." What would we think of a sun that could not shine? What would we think of a God who does not shine? Not much, but God does shine! God is light! Take time, just be still, and rest in the light of God. The eyes are feeble, and the windows are not clean, but determine to *wait on the Lord.* The light does shine, the light will shine in you and make you full of light. And you will learn to walk all day in the light and joy of God. Then you too will proclaim, "My soul waits for the Lord more than those who watch for the morning."

"My soul, wait only on God!"

Personal Reflection

Day 17

In Times of Darkness

"I will wait on the Lord, who hides His face from the house of Jacob; and I will hope in Him."—Isaiah 8:17

Here we have a servant of God who is waiting on the Lord, not on behalf of himself, but on behalf of his people from whom God was hiding His face. This suggests to us that though our waiting on God may begin with our personal needs and with our desire for God to reveal Himself to us, it must not stop there. We may be walking in the full light of God's countenance, yet God may be hiding His face from the people around us. We can remain content, thinking that this is simply the just punishment of their sin, or the consequence of their indifference; but we are called to be tender hearted, to mourn their sad estate and to wait on God on their behalf. The privilege of waiting on God brings great responsibility. Christ, when He entered God's presence and assumed the highest place of privilege and honor, became our intercessor; so we too, when we enter in and wait on God, must use our access on behalf of those less favored. "I will wait on the Lord, who hides His face from the house of Jacob."

Perhaps you worship with a certain congregation and do not find the spiritual life or joy that you desire either in the preaching or in the fellowship. You also belong to the larger denomination, with its many congregations. But there you observe so much of error and worldliness, of reliance on human wisdom and culture, of trust in ordinances and observances, that you do not wonder that God hides His face. In many cases, there is little power for conversion or true edification. Then there are branches of Christian work to which you are connected—a Christian school, a gospel band, a youth ministry, a mission work—in which the absence of the Spirit's working indicates that God is hiding His face. You think you know the reason. There is too much trust in personnel and money; there is too much formality and self-indulgence; there is too little faith and prayer; too little love and humility; too little of the spirit of the crucified Jesus. At times you feel as if things are hopeless; nothing will help.

Do believe that God can help and will help. Adopt the spirit of the prophet, as you receive his words and commit to waiting on God on behalf of His erring children. Instead of falling into judgment or condemnation, despondency or despair, accept your calling to wait on God. If others fail to do so, redouble your efforts. The deeper the darkness, the greater the need of appealing to the Light. The greater the self-sufficiency around you (which doesn't realize that it is poor and wretched and blind), the more urgent the call is to those who see the evil and have access to Him who alone can help. Remain at your post, *waiting on God*. Whenever you are tempted to complain or to sigh, say instead: "I will wait on the Lord, who hides His face from the house of Jacob."

There is a still larger circle, the Christian church throughout the world. Think of all the Orthodox, Catholic, and Protestant churches, and the state of the millions that belong to them. There is much nominal professionalism and formality in the temple of God. Is that not abundant proof that God does hide His face!

So, what are those who see and mourn the sad state of the church supposed to do? The first thing to be done is this: "I will wait on the Lord, who hides His face from the house of Jacob." Let us wait on God, in humble confession of the sins of His people. Let us set aside time and wait on Him in this exercise. Let us wait on God in tender, loving intercession for all saints, our beloved family, however wrong their lives or their teaching may appear. Let us wait on God in faith and expectation, until we sense that He has heard. Let us wait on God, with the simple offering of ourselves to his purposes, and the earnest prayer that He would revive His church. Let us wait on God as Isaiah urged, "and give Him no rest till He makes Jerusalem a joy in the earth" (Isaiah 62:7). Yes, let us turn to the Lord and wait patiently for Him who now hides His face from so many of His children. And let us say regarding the light of His countenance, which we long for all His people to see: "I wait for the Lord, my soul waits, and in His word do I hope. My soul waits for the Lord more than those who watch for the morning, yes, more than those who watch for the morning."

"My soul, wait only on God!"

Personal Reflection

Day 18

To Reveal Himself

"And it will be said in that day: Behold, this is our God;
we have waited for Him, and He will save us. this is the
Lord; we have waited for Him, we will be glad and rejoice
in His salvation."—Isaiah 25:9

In this passage, we have two precious thoughts. One is that
this is the language of God's people who have been waiting
unitedly on Him; the second is that in response to their waiting
God revealed Himself. So, they can joyfully say, "BEHOLD,
THIS IS OUR GOD....THIS IS THE LORD." The power
and the blessing of united waiting is something we need to
learn. Note the twice repeated phrase, "We have waited for
Him." In a time of trouble, the hearts of the people had been
drawn together and, forsaking all human hope or help, they
had with one heart gathered to wait for their God.

Is not this just what we need in our churches and
conventions and prayer meetings? Is there not great enough
need in the church and the world to demand it? Certainly, there
are evils in the church of Christ that no human wisdom can
equal. Ritualism and rationalism, formalism and worldliness,
are robbing the church of its power. Culture and money and
pleasure are threatening its spiritual life. Are the powers of the
church utterly inadequate to cope with the powers of infidelity
and iniquity and wretchedness in our country and around the
world? Is there not, in the promise of God and in the power
of the Holy Spirit, provision enough to meet this great need?
How can the church rest in the assurance that she is doing all

that God expects of her? Most certainly, only united waiting on God for the supply of His Spirit will bring the needed help and blessing. We cannot doubt it.

The aim of more intentional waiting on God in our gatherings would be much the same as in personal practice. It would require the same prayerful posture: a deep conviction that God must and will do all; a humble and abiding admission of our deep helplessness, of entire and unceasing dependence on Him; a constant awareness that the essential thing is to give God His place of honor and power; a confident expectation that to those who wait on Him, God will reveal the secret of His acceptance and presence, and, in due time, the revelation of His saving power. The great aim would be to bring everyone in a praying and worshipping company under a deep sense of God's presence, so that when they part it will be with the consciousness of having met God Himself, of having left every request with Him, and of now resting in the assurance of His salvation.

It is this type of experience that is celebrated in our text. The fulfillment of the words may, at times, be in such striking demonstrations of God's power that all can join in the cry, "BEHOLD, THIS IS OUR GOD; THIS IS THE LORD!" They may equally be fulfilled in spiritual experience, when God's people in their waiting become so conscious of His presence that in holy awe they proclaim, "BEHOLD, THIS IS OUR GOD; THIS IS THE LORD!" It is this sense of awe that is too often missing when we meet for worship. The godly minister has no more difficult, no more solemn, no more blessed task, than to lead the people out to meet God, and, even before preaching a sermon, to bring each one into contact with God. "Now therefore, we are all present before God" (Acts 10:33). These words of Cornelius show how Peter's audience was prepared for the coming of the Holy Spirit. Waiting before God, waiting for God, waiting on God—these are the preconditions of God for revealing His presence.

If only a company of believers would gather together for the sole purpose of helping each other to wait on God alone, by intervals of silence opening the heart for whatever God may reveal—whether that be a disclosure of sin, of His will, of new areas for ministry, or of new ways of doing things. Those gathered would soon have reason to exclaim, "BEHOLD, THIS IS OUR GOD; we have waited for Him, He shall save us: THIS IS THE LORD; we have waited for Him, we will be glad and rejoice in His salvation."

"My soul, wait only on God!"

Personal Reflection

Day 19

The God of Judgment

"Yes, in the way of Your judgments, O Lord,
we have waited for You: for when Your judgments
are in the earth, the inhabitants of the world will
learn righteousness."—Isaiah 26:8-9

"The Lord is a God of justice; blessed are all those
who wait for Him."—Isaiah 30:18

The Lord is a God of both mercy and judgment. Mercy and judgment always are found together in His dealings with humankind. In the devastation of the flood, in the deliverance of Israel out of Egypt, in the overthrow of the Canaanites, we find mercy even during severe judgment. Within the inner circle of God's own people, we see it, too: the judgment that punishes the sin, while mercy saves the sinner. Or, rather, mercy saves the sinner, not in spite of the sin but rather by means of the very judgment for that sin. In waiting on God, we must not forget this: as we wait on God, we must expect Him to bring judgment.

"In the way of Your judgments, we have waited for You." That will prove true in our inner experience. If we are honest in our longing for holiness, in our prayer to be wholly the Lord's, His holy presence will discover hidden sin and bring us under bitter conviction of the evil in our nature, its opposition to God's law and its impotence to fulfill that law. These words will ring true: "But who can endure the day of His coming, for He is like a refiner's fire" (Malachi 3:2). "Oh, that You would rend the heavens! That you would come down! That the mountains might shake at Your presence" (Isaiah 64:1). In great mercy God executes His judgment on sin within the soul, as He makes it feel its wickedness and guilt. Many will try to flee from this judgment: but the soul that longs for God and for deliverance from sin bows down in humility and in hope. In silence of soul it says, "In the way of Your judgments we have waited for You. Rise up, O Lord! Let Your enemies be scattered" (Numbers 10:35).

Don't be surprised if your first attempts to learn the blessed art of waiting on God only reveal more of your sin and darkness. And don't despair if unconquered sins or evil thoughts or great darkness appear to hide God's face. Even the beloved Son, the gift and bearer of divine mercy on Calvary, felt hidden from God and lost in judgment. Simply submit to the judgment of your every sin, for judgment paves the way to wonderful mercy. It is written, "Zion shall be redeemed with justice" (Isaiah 1:27). Wait on God, believing that His tender mercy is working out your redemption by way of judgment: wait for Him to be gracious to you.

There is another application, one of great solemnity. We are expecting God to visit this earth in the way of His judgments; we are waiting for Him to do so. What a thought! We know of these coming judgments; we also know that there are tens of thousands of professing Christians who live carelessly, and who might suffer judgment if they don't change their ways. We must do all we can to warn them, to plead with and for them, that God may have mercy on them.

If we sense a lack of boldness or zeal or power, then we need to wait on God even more definitely and persistently as the God of judgment. We can even ask Him to reveal Himself in the judgments that are coming on our friends, so that we may be inspired with a new fear of Him, and be constrained to speak and pray for them as never before. Truly, waiting on God is not meant for spiritual self-indulgence. Its purpose is to let God and His holiness, Christ and the love that died on Calvary, the Spirit and the fire that came from heaven, take hold of us, to warn and rouse others with the message that we are waiting for God to come in the way of His judgments. Oh, Christian, prove that you really believe in the God of judgment.

"My soul, wait only on God!"

Personal Reflection

Day 20

Who Waits on Us

"Therefore the Lord will wait, that He may be gracious to you; and therefore He will be exalted, that He may have mercy on you. For the Lord is a God of justice; blessed are all those who wait for Him."—Isaiah 30:18

We must think not only of our waiting on God, but also of what is more wonderful still, of God's waiting on us. The vision of Him waiting on us will give new inspiration to our waiting on Him. It will give us an unshakeable confidence that our waiting cannot be in vain. If He waits for us, then we can be sure that we are more than welcome; that He rejoices to find those He has been seeking. Even now, at this moment, in the spirit of lowly waiting on God, let us discover something of what this means: "Therefore the Lord will wait, that he may be gracious to you." Let us accept and echo back the message: "Blessed are all those who wait for Him."

Look up and see the great God upon His throne. He is Love—Love with an unceasing and inexpressible desire to communicate His goodness and blessing to all His creatures. He longs and delights to bless. He has inconceivably glorious purposes concerning every one of His children, which he longs to reveal in them by the power of His Holy Spirit. He waits with the ache of a father's heart. He waits that He may be gracious to you. So, each time you come before Him or practice in daily life the holy habit of waiting on God, look up and envision Him ready to meet you, waiting that He may be gracious to you. Yes, connect every exercise, every breath of the life of waiting, with faith's vision of your Father waiting for you.

You may wonder, why is it, that after I come and wait on Him, it seems He waits even longer to be gracious and does not give the help I seek? There is a double answer. One reason is this: God is like the wise farmer, who "waits for the precious fruit of the earth, waiting patiently for it" (James 5:7). Just as the farmer cannot gather the fruit until it is ripe, God knows when we are spiritually ready to reap the blessing for our greatest profit and His glory. Waiting in the sunshine of His love is what will ripen the soul for His blessing. Waiting under the cloud of trial, which breaks in showers of blessing, is also necessary. Be assured that if God waits longer than you wish, it is only to make the blessing twice as precious. God waited four thousand years, until the fullness of time, before He sent His Son. Scripture assures us, "My times are in His hands" (Psalm 31:15). And as Jesus declared regarding God's elect, "He will avenge them speedily" (Luke 18:8). God will come quickly to our defense, and not delay one hour too long.

The second reason why God waits has been stated before. The giver is more than the gift; God is more than the blessing; and our being kept waiting on Him is the only way we learn to find our life and joy in God Himself. Oh, if God's children only knew what a wonderful Father they have, and what a privilege it is to enjoy fellowship with Him! Then they would rejoice in His presence, even when He keeps them waiting for his gifts. They would learn to understand better than ever this truth: "Therefore the Lord will wait, that He may be gracious to you." His waiting would then be the highest proof of His love.

"Blessed are all those who wait for Him." A queen has her ladies-in-waiting. The position is one of subordination and service, and yet it is considered one of high dignity and privilege, because a wise and gracious sovereign makes them her companions and friends. What a dignity and privilege it is to be attendants-in-waiting on the Everlasting God, ever watchful for any indication of His will or favor, ever conscious of His nearness, His goodness and His grace! "The Lord is good to those who wait for Him" (Lamentations 3:24). "Blessed are all those who wait for Him." How wonderful it is when a waiting soul and a waiting God meet each other! God cannot do His work without it being the right time: so let waiting be our work, just as it is His, for that right time. And if our God be nothing but goodness and grace, let our waiting be nothing but a rejoicing in that goodness, and a confident expectancy of that grace. And, let every moment of waiting become to us the experience of unmingled and unspeakable blessedness, because it brings us before the God who waits to make Himself perfectly known to us as the Gracious One.

"My soul, wait only on God!"

Personal Reflection

Day 21

The Almighty One

"But those who wait on the Lord shall renew their
strength; they shall mount up with wings like eagles, they
shall run and not be weary, they shall walk and not faint."
—Isaiah 40:31

Our waiting always takes into account our opinion of the
one on whom we wait. Our waiting on God will depend
greatly on our idea of what He is. This well-known passage
from Isaiah 40 reveals God as the Everlasting and Almighty
One. As that revelation enters our soul, our waiting will
become the spontaneous expression of what we know Him to
be—a God most worthy to be waited on. Review this passage
with me:

"Why do you say, O Jacob, and speak, O Israel: 'My way is
hidden from the Lord, and my just claim is passed over by my
God'? [Why speak as though God does not hear or help?]

"Have you not known? Have you not heard? The everlasting
God, the Lord, the Creator of the ends of the earth, neither
faints nor is weary. [Far from it!]

"He gives power to the weak, and to those who have no might
He increases strength. Even the youths shall faint and be weary,
and the young men shall utterly fall. [All that men count on for
their strength will fail.] But those who wait on the Lord [on the
everlasting God, who neither faints nor is weary] shall renew
their strength; they shall mount up with wings like eagles; they
shall run and [listen now, they shall be strong with the strength

of God] and not be weary [even as He]; they shall walk and [even as He] not faint" (Isaiah 40:27-31).

Yes, "they shall mount up with wings like eagles." You know what "wings like eagles" mean? The eagle is the king of birds; it soars the highest into the heavens. Believers are to live a heavenly life, in the very presence and love and joy of God. They are to live where God lives; but they need God's strength to rise there. To those who wait on Him that strength shall be given.

How are eagles' wings obtained? Only in one way—by the eagle's birth. If you are born of God, you too have wings like eagles. You may not have known it, you may not have used them; but God can and will teach you how to use them.

Perhaps you know how young eagles are taught the use of their wings. Imagine a cliff rising a thousand feet out of the sea. Allow your eyes to travel high up to a rocky ledge on which is perched an eagle's nest with its treasure of two young eaglets. Then observe the mother bird come and stir up her nest, and with her beak push the timid birds over the precipice. See how they flutter and fall and sink toward the depth. See then how the parent "hovers over its young, spreading out its wings, taking them up, carrying them on its wings" (Deuteronomy 32:11). And so, as they ride upon her wings, she brings them to a place of safety. The eagle does this over and over again, each time casting its young out over the precipice, then catching and carrying them to safety. "So the Lord alone led him" (Deuteronomy 32:12). The instinct of the parent eagle is God's gift, a single ray of that love by which the Almighty trains His people to rise up as on wings like eagles.

God stirs up your nest. He disappoints your hopes. He brings down your confidence. He makes you fear and tremble. All your strength fails, and you feel utterly weary and helpless.

Yet all the while He is spreading His strong wings for you to rest your weakness upon, and offering His everlasting strength to work for you. All He asks is that you sink down in your weariness and wait on Him, allowing Him to carry you as you ride upon the wings of His omnipotence.

Dear child of God, I encourage you to raise your head and behold your God. Listen to Him who "neither faints nor is weary," who promises that you too shall not faint or be weary, who asks nothing but this one thing, that you should wait on Him. Oh, will you not do what God asks, just be quiet and let Him work? Let your answer be: For such a God, so mighty, so faithful, so tender, I will wait.

"My soul, wait only on God!"

Personal Reflection

Day 22

The Certainty of Blessing

"For they shall not be ashamed who wait for Me."
—Isaiah 49:23

"Blessed are all those who wait for Him."
—Isaiah 30:18

What promises! God seeks to draw us into waiting on Him by the most positive assurance that it will not be in vain: "They shall not be ashamed who wait for Me." How strange then, that we who so often have experienced it are yet so slow to understand that this blessed waiting must and can be the very breath of our life, a continuous resting in God's presence and love, a continual yielding of ourselves to His perfect work in us. Let us once again listen and meditate, until our heart says with new conviction: "Blessed are all those who wait for Him!" On Day 6 we examined the prayer of Psalm 25: "Let no one who waits on You be ashamed." This prayer reveals what we fear— being ashamed. We need to repeat God's assurances, until every fear is banished and we send back to heaven the very words of God. Yes, Lord, we believe what You have said: "They shall not be ashamed who wait for me" and "Blessed are all those who wait for Him."

The context of these two passages points us to times when God's people were in dire straits; to the human mind there was no possibility of deliverance. But God intervened with this word of promise and with the pledge of almighty power for the deliverance of His people. As the God who had Himself undertaken the work of their redemption, He invited them to wait on Him and assured them that disappointment was impossible.

The church today is in a dire state, with its profession and its formalism. Along with all we praise God for, there is, unfortunately, much to mourn over. If not for God's promises, we might easily despair. But in His promises the Living God has bound Himself to us. He calls us to wait on Him. He assures us we shall not be put to shame. Oh, that our hearts might learn to wait before Him, until He reveals to us what those promises mean and in those promises reveals His hidden glory! Then we would be irresistibly drawn to wait on Him alone. May God increase the company of those who say, "Our soul waits for the Lord; He is our help and our shield" (Psalm 33:20).

This waiting on God on behalf of the church will depend largely on the place that waiting on Him has taken in our personal life. The mind may have beautiful visions of what God has promised to do, and the lips may speak of them in stirring words, but these are not really the measure of our faith or power. No, it is what we really know of God in our personal experience, conquering the enemies within, reigning and ruling, revealing Himself in holiness and power in our inmost being. This will be the real measure of the spiritual blessing we expect from Him and in turn bring to others. Only when we can acknowledge how blessed the waiting on God has become to our own souls, can we confidently hope in the same blessing to come on the church around us.

The keyword of all our expectations will be the promise: "They shall not be ashamed who wait on Me." Because of all He has done in us personally, we trust Him to do mighty things around us. "Blessed are all those who wait for Him." Yes, they are blessed even now in the waiting. The promised blessings, for ourselves or for others, may tarry; yet the blessedness of knowing Him who has promised, the living fountain of the coming blessings, is even now ours. Allow this truth to take hold in your soul; that waiting on God is itself the highest privilege of the creature, the highest blessedness of His redeemed child.

Even as the sunshine enters with its light and warmth, with its beauty and blessing, into every little blade of grass that rises out of the cold earth, so the Everlasting God enters with the tenderness of His love into the heart of each waiting child. We have "the light of the knowledge of the glory of God in the face of Jesus Christ" (2 Corinthians 4:6). Read these words again, until your heart grasps what God waits to do to you. Who can measure the difference between the great sun and that little blade of grass? And yet the grass has all the sunlight it can need or hold. Do believe that in waiting on God, His greatness and your smallness suit and meet each other most wonderfully. Just bow in emptiness and poverty and utter impotence; in humility and meekness simply surrender to His will. And be still. As you wait on Him, God draws near. He will reveal Himself as the God who will fulfill mightily His every promise. And then may your heart take up the song: "Blessed are all those who wait for Him."

"My soul, wait only on God!"

Personal Reflection

Day 23

For Unlooked-For Things

"For since the beginning of the world men have not heard
nor perceived by the ear, nor has the eye seen any God
besides You, who acts for the one who waits for Him."
—Isaiah 64:4

The text says: "Men have not heard . . . nor has the eye
seen *any God besides You*," referring to our matchless God.
A related thought is that no one has ever heard or seen "any
God besides You, *who acts*," referring to the wonderful things
that God does on behalf of those who wait for Him. In both
thoughts the common idea is that our role is to wait on God,
and then it will be revealed to us what the human heart cannot
conceive. The apostle Paul quotes this passage a bit differently,
referring to those things that the Holy Spirit is to reveal: "Eye
has not seen, nor ear heard, nor have entered into the heart
of man the things which God has prepared for those who love
Him" (1 Corinthians 2:9).

Previous verses from Isaiah 63 describe the lowly state of
God's people. The prayer has been poured out, "Look down
from heaven" (v. 15). "Why have you made us stray from your
way, and hardened our heart from Your fear? Return for Your
servants' sake" (v. 17). Next comes the still more urgent cry,
"Oh, that You would rend the heavens! That You would come
down!... To make Your name known to Your adversaries!"
Then follows a reminder from the past, "When You did
awesome things for which we did not look, You came down.
The mountains shook at Your presence" (Isaiah 64:1-3).

"When you did awesome things"— now faith is awakened by the memory of unexpected things God had done, "things for which we did not look." He is still the same God "who acts for the one who waits for Him." God alone knows what He can do for His waiting people. As Paul explains it: "No one knows the things of God, except the Spirit of God. But God has revealed them to us through His Spirit" (1 Corinthians 2:10, 11).

The need of God's people, and the call for God's intervention, is as urgent in our day as it was in the time of Isaiah. There is now, as there was then, a remnant that seek after God with their whole heart. But, if we look at Christendom as a whole, at the state of the church of Christ, there is infinite cause for begging God to rend the heavens and come down. Nothing but a special outpouring of almighty power will help. I fear we have no conception of what the so-called Christian world looks like in the sight of God. Unless God comes down "as fire burns brushwood, as fire causes water to boil" to make His name known to His adversaries, our labors are comparatively fruitless (Isaiah 64:2). Look at any ministry; so much is done in the wisdom of man and of literary culture, and so little is done in the council of the Spirit and of power. Think of the unity of the Body; how little evidence there is of a heavenly love that binds God's children into one. Think of holiness, the holiness of Christlike humility in the crucifixion; how little the world sees the Christ of heaven in those Christians that live among them.

What is to be done? There is but one thing. We must wait on God. And what do we wait for? We must cry, with a cry that never stops, "Oh, that You would rend the heavens and come down, that the mountains might shake at Your presence." We must desire and believe, we must ask and expect, that God will do unlooked-for things. We must set our faith on God and look for "the things which God has prepared for those who love Him." The wonder-working God, who can surpass all our expectations, must be the God of our confidence.

Let us as God's people enlarge our hearts to wait on "Him who is able to do exceedingly abundantly above all that we ask or think, according to the power that works in us" (Ephesians 3:20). Let us band ourselves together as the elect who cry day and night for God to do things eyes have not yet seen. He will come down and make His name known. "The Lord will wait, that He may be gracious to you; blessed are all those who wait for Him" (Isaiah 30:18).

"My soul, wait only on God!"

Personal Reflection

Day 24

To Know His Goodness

"The Lord is good to those who wait for Him,
to the soul who seeks Him."—Lamentations 3:25

Scripture proclaims the goodness of God: "No one is good but One, that is God" (Matthew 19:17). "Oh, how great is Your goodness, which You have laid up for those who fear You, which you have prepared for those who trust in you!" (Psalm 31:19). "Oh, taste and see that the Lord is good!" (Psalm 34:8). This is the true way of entering into and rejoicing in this goodness of God—waiting on Him. The Lord is good—even when His children do not know it, for they do not wait in quietness for Him to reveal it. But to those who persevere in waiting, whose souls do wait, it will come true. One might think that those who are made to wait a long time would doubt the goodness of God. But that only happens when they do not wait but grow impatient. The truly waiting ones will say, "The Lord is good to those who wait for Him." If you would truly like to know the goodness of God, then commit yourself more than ever to a life of waiting on Him.

When we first enter the school of waiting on God, our primary focus is on the blessings that we seek. But God graciously uses our needs and desires to help educate us to look for something higher than we were thinking. We were seeking gifts; He, the Giver, longs to give Himself and to satisfy the soul with His goodness. It is for this very reason that He often withholds the gifts and makes the time of waiting so long. He is always seeking to win the heart of His child. He desires that we should not only say when we receive a gift, "How good is God!" But that long before the gift comes, and even if it never comes, we should always say: "It is *good* that one should hope and wait quietly. The Lord is *good* to those who wait for Him."

What a blessed life the life of waiting then becomes, the continual worship of faith, adoring and trusting His goodness. As the soul learns its secret, every act or exercise of waiting just becomes *a quiet entering into the goodness of God*, to let it do its blessed work and satisfy our every need. And every experience of God's goodness gives the work of waiting new attractiveness; instead of only taking refuge in time of need, there comes a great longing to wait continually and all the day. No matter what duties and engagements occupy the time and the mind, the soul gets more familiar with the secret art of always waiting. Waiting becomes the habit and disposition, the very second nature and breath of the soul.

Are you beginning to see that waiting is not one among many Christian virtues, to be practiced from time to time, but that it expresses that disposition which lies at the very root of the Christian life? It gives a higher value and a new power to our prayer and worship, to our faith and surrender, because it links us in unalterable dependence to God Himself. And it gives us the unbroken enjoyment of the goodness of God: "The Lord is good to those who wait for Him."

Let me urge you once again to take the time to cultivate this so much needed element of the Christian life. We get too much of religion second hand from the teaching of others. That teaching has great value if it leads us to God Himself, even as the preaching of John the Baptist directed his disciples away from himself to the Living Christ. What our faith needs is—*more of God*. Many of us are too much occupied with our work. As with Martha, the very service we want to render the Master separates us from Him; it is neither pleasing to

Him nor profitable to ourselves. The more work we do, the more we need to wait on God. Doing God's will, instead of being exhausting would then become our meat and drink, our nourishment and refreshment. "The Lord is good to those who wait for Him." How good no one can tell but those who prove it by waiting on Him.

"My soul, wait only on God!"

Personal Reflection

Day 25

Waiting Quietly

"It is good that one should hope and wait quietly for the salvation of the Lord."—Lamentations 3:26

Let us focus today on the God of our salvation: "Take heed, and be quiet: do not fear or be fainthearted" (Isaiah 7:4). "In quietness and confidence shall be your strength" (Isaiah 30:15). Verses such as those above reveal to us the close connection between quietness and faith; they show us what a deep need there is of quietness as an element of true waiting on God. If we are to turn our whole heart toward God, then we must first turn it away from ourselves, from all that occupies and interests, whether of joy or sorrow.

God is a being of such infinite greatness and glory, and our nature has become so estranged from his likeness, that we need to set our whole mind and heart on Him, even in some little measure, to know and receive Him. Everything that is not God, anything that excites our fears or stirs our efforts or awakens our hopes or makes us glad, hinders our perfect waiting on Him. The message to wait quietly has deep meaning: "In quietness and confidence shall be your strength."

The very thought of God in His majesty and holiness should silence us, as scripture abundantly testifies:

"The Lord is in His holy temple; let all the earth keep silence before Him" (Habakkuk 2:20).

"Be silent in the presence of the Lord God" (Zephaniah 1:7).

"Be silent, all flesh, before the Lord; for He is aroused from His holy habitation" (Zechariah 2:13).

As long as we regard waiting on God as the means toward more effectual prayer with the end of obtaining our petitions, this state of perfect quietness will never be achieved. But, once we realize that waiting on God is itself an unspeakable blessing and one of the highest forms of fellowship with the Holy One, then the adoration of God in His glory will of necessity humble the soul into holy stillness, making way for God to speak and reveal Himself. The precious promise is thus fulfilled, that all of self and self-effort shall be humbled: "The haughtiness of men shall be bowed down, and the Lord alone shall be exalted in that day" (Isaiah 2:11).

Anyone who would learn the art of waiting on God should remember the lesson: "Take heed and be quiet." Take time away from all friends and all duties, all cares and all joys; take time to be still and quiet before God. Take time not only to be separate from other people and activity, but also from self and its energy. Let scripture and prayer be very precious; but remember, even these may hinder the quiet waiting. The activity of the mind in studying scripture or giving expression to its thoughts in prayer, the activity of the heart with its desires and hopes and fears–these activities may so engage us that we do not come into the still waiting on the All-Glorious One. Our whole being is not bowed in silence before Him. Though at first it will be difficult to wait quietly, with the activities of mind and heart for a time subdued, every effort to do so will be rewarded. You will find that it grows upon you, and that a little season of silent worship brings a peace and a rest that blesses you not only during prayer, but all the day.

"It is good that one should hope and wait quietly for the salvation of the Lord." Yes, *it is good*. "So then, it is not of him who wills, nor of him who runs, but of God who shows mercy"

(Romans 9:16). The quietness is the confession of our impotence, that with all our willing and running, with all our thinking and praying, we cannot work our salvation; we must receive it from God. It is the confession of our trust that God will come to our help in good time. It is the confession of our desire to sink into our nothingness, the quiet resting in God alone to let Him work and reveal Himself. Let us wait quietly. In daily life let there be a quiet reverence, a watchfulness against too deep engrossment with the world. And the soul that waits for God to do His wondrous work, the whole character will come to bear this beautiful stamp: Quietly waiting for the salvation of God.

"My soul, wait only on God!"

Personal Reflection

Day 26

In Holy Expectation

"Therefore I will look to the Lord; I will wait for the God of my salvation; my God will hear me."—Micah 7:7

There is a beautiful little story, *Expectation Corner*, which provides one of the best sermons on our text. It tells of a king who built a city for some of his poor subjects. Not far from the city were large storehouses, where everything they could possibly need was supplied. They only had to send in their requests. There was but one condition—that they should be on the lookout for the answer, so that when the king's messengers came with the requested supplies, they would always be found waiting and ready to receive them. The sad story is told of one despondent subject who never expected to get what he asked, he considered himself too unworthy. One day he was taken to the king's storehouses and there, to his amazement, he saw a stack of packages bearing his address, packages that had been made up for him and sent. There was the garment of praise and the oil of joy and the eye salve, and so much more. The king's messengers had been to his door but had found it closed; the man had not been on the lookout. In that moment he learned the lesson Micah would teach us today: "I will look to the Lord; I will wait for the God of my salvation; my God will hear me."

I have said more than once: Waiting for the answer to prayer is not the whole of waiting, but only a part. Today I want to explore this blessed truth: It is only a part, but a very important one. When we are waiting on God regarding a

126

special petition, our waiting must be in the confident assurance that "My God will hear me." A holy, joyful expectancy is the very essence of true waiting. This not only refers to the many varied requests every believer makes, but most especially to the one great petition that every heart should seek for itself—that THE LIFE OF GOD in the soul may have full sway; that Christ may be fully formed within; that we may be filled to all the fullness of God. This is what God has promised. This is what God's people seek too little, very often because they do not believe it possible. This is what we ought to seek and dare to expect, because God is able and waiting to work it in us.

But GOD HIMSELF must work it. And for this reason our working must cease. We must trust entirely in the operation of God who raised Jesus from the dead. Just as much as the resurrection was the work of God, so the perfecting of our souls must be entirely His work. And our waiting has to become more than ever a tarrying before God in stillness of soul, counting on Him "who gives life to the dead and calls those things which do not exist as though they did" (Romans 4:17).

Just notice how the threefold use of the name of God in our text points us to Himself as the one from whom alone is our expectation. "I will look to THE LORD; I will wait for THE GOD OF MY SALVATION; MY GOD will hear me." Everything about our salvation, everything that is good and holy, must be the direct mighty work of God Himself within us. In every moment of life spent in the will of God we can expect the immediate operation of God. The one thing I have to do is this: to look to the Lord; to wait for the God of my salvation; to hold fast the confident assurance, "My God will hear me."

The Lord says: "Be still, and know that I am God" (Psalm 46:10). There is no stillness like that of the grave. In the grave of Jesus, in the fellowship of His death, in the death of oneself with its own will and wisdom, its own strength and energy, there is rest. As we cease from self, and our soul becomes still to God, God will arise and show Himself. First "be still," and then you shall "know that I am God." There is no stillness like the quiet Jesus gives when He speaks, "Peace, be still!" (Mark 4:39). In Christ, in His death and in His life, in His perfected redemption, the soul may be still; and God will come in and take possession and do His perfect work.

"My soul, wait only on God!"

Personal Reflection

Day 27

For Redemption

"Simeon ... was just and devout, waiting for the
consolation of Israel, and the Holy Spirit was upon him.
... Anna, a prophetess, ... spoke of Him to all those who
looked for redemption in Jerusalem."—Luke 2:25, 36, 38

Here we have the marks of a waiting believer. Simeon was
"just," righteous in all his conduct; "devout," devoted to
God; "waiting for the consolation of Israel," looking for the
fulfillment of God's promises; "and the Holy Spirit was upon
him," he radiated the presence of God. In devout waiting
he had been prepared for the coming blessing of Jesus. And
Simeon was not the only one. Anna came upon the scene
and "in that instant" recognized the child as the Christ
and thereafter "spoke of him to all those who looked for
redemption in Jerusalem." This was the distinguishing mark,
amidst a religious yet worldly society, of a godly band of men
and women in Jerusalem. They were waiting on God, looking
for His promised redemption.

Now that the Consolation of Israel has come, and our
redemption has been accomplished, do we still need to wait? We
do indeed. But our waiting, as we look back to our Redeemer
as having come, will differ greatly from those who looked
forward to His coming. It will differ especially in two ways: We
now wait on God in the full power of our redemption, and we
wait for its full revelation in us.

We now wait in the full power of our redemption. Christ said, "You are already clean.... Abide in Me, and I in you" (John 15:3-4). The Epistles teach us to consider ourselves "dead indeed to sin, but alive to God in Christ Jesus our Lord" (Romans 6:11). "God has blessed us with every spiritual blessing in the heavenly places in Christ" (Ephesians 1:3). Our waiting on God is now with the wonderful consciousness, made possible by the Holy Spirit within us, that we are "accepted in the Beloved" (Ephesians 1:6). The love that rests on the Son also rests on us. We are living in that love, in the very nearness and presence and sight of God. The saints of old took their stand on the word of God and waited, hoping on that word; we stand on the word too—but, with much greater privilege, as one with Christ Jesus. In our waiting on God, this is our confidence: In Christ we have access to the Father; therefore, we can be sure that our waiting is not in vain.

Our waiting also differs in this, that while they waited for a redemption to come, we see it accomplished and now wait for its revelation in us. Christ not only said, "Abide in Me," but also "and *I in you*." The Epistles not only speak of us in Christ, but also of Christ *in us*, as the highest mystery of redeeming love. As we maintain our place in Christ day by day, God begins to reveal Christ in us. This is done in such a way that He is formed in us; His mind and disposition and likeness acquire form and substance in us, so that it may be said, "it is no longer I who live, but Christ lives in me" (Galatians 2:20).

My life in Christ up there in heaven and Christ's life in me down here on earth—these two complement each other. And the more my waiting on God is marked by the faith that *I am in Christ*, the more the heart thirsts for and claims the Christ who *lives in me*. My waiting on God, which began with special needs and prayer, will increasingly be concentrated, as far as my personal life is concerned, on this one thing: Lord, reveal Your redemption fully in me; let Christ live in me.

We can learn another lesson from Simeon and Anna. Think of how utterly impossible it was for them to do anything to bring about their redemption. The birth of Christ, His life, death and resurrection—it was all God's work. They could do nothing but wait for it. We are just as helpless to bring about the revelation of Christ in us. God did not work out His great plan of redemption in Christ, then leave the details of its application to us. The false belief that this is so lies at the root of all our feebleness. Rather, the daily revelation of Christ in the individual believer, step by step and moment by moment, is as much the work of God's omnipotence as was the birth or resurrection of Christ. Let this truth take root in our minds and fill our hearts, then we will know that we are just as dependent on God in our present enjoyment of redemption as they were in their faithful anticipation of it. Our waiting on God in each moment of our life will then bring its full blessing.

Our waiting differs from that of the saints of old both in the place we stand, and in the expectations we entertain. But at root it is the same: waiting on God, who alone is our hope and consolation. The sense of utter and absolute helplessness, the confidence that God can and will do all—these are the marks of all who have ever waited on God. And as gloriously as God proved Himself to the saints of old, so will this faithful and wonder-working God prove Himself to us too.

"My soul, wait only on God!"

Personal Reflection

Day 28

For the Coming of His Son

"You yourselves be like men who wait for their master."
—Luke 12:36

"Until our Lord Jesus Christ's appearing, which He will
manifest in His own time, He who is the blessed and only
Potentate, the King of kings and Lord of lords."
—1 Timothy 6:14-15

"You turned to God from idols to serve the living and
true God, and to wait for His Son from heaven."
—1 Thessalonians 1:9-10

Waiting on God in heaven, and waiting for His Son from heaven, these two disciplines God has joined together and may no one put them asunder. The waiting on God for His presence and power in daily life will be the only true preparation for waiting for Christ in humility and holiness. The waiting for Christ's coming from heaven to take us to heaven will give the waiting on God its true tone of hopefulness and joy. The Father who in His own time will reveal His Son from heaven is the God who, as we wait on Him, prepares us for the revelation of His Son. The present life and the coming glory are inseparably connected in God and in us.

There is sometimes a danger of separating them. It is always easier to be engaged with the religion of the past or with the promise of the future than to be faithful in the religion of today. So, while we are looking at what God has done in the past or looking for what God will do in the future, we may actually be avoiding the personal claim of present duty and present submission to His will. Waiting on God must always lead to waiting for Christ as the glorious consummation of His work; and waiting for Christ must always remind us of our present duty of waiting on God. Our faithful waiting on God is the only proof that our waiting for Christ is done "in spirit and in truth" (John 4:24). There is a real danger of our being more occupied with *the things* that are coming than *with Him* who is to come. There is such scope for imagination and reason and human ingenuity in the study of coming events, that nothing but humble waiting on God can save us from mistaking the interest and pleasure of intellectual study for the true love of Christ and His appearing. All you who are waiting for Christ's coming, make sure that you are also waiting on God now. All you who are waiting on God now to reveal His Son in you, make sure that you are also waiting for the revelation of His Son from heaven. The hope of that glorious appearing is what inspires us to wait on God to do His work in our hearts: and the same omnipotent love working to prepare our hearts even now is planning that glorious reveal.

"The blessed hope and glorious appearing of our great God and Savior Jesus Christ" (Titus 2:13),is one of the great bonds of union given to the church throughout the ages. "He comes, in that Day, to be glorified in His saints and to be admired among all those who believe" (2 Thessalonians 1:10)."In that Day" we shall all meet, and the unity of the body of Christ will be seen in its divine glory. It will be the meeting place and the triumph of divine love: Jesus receiving His own and presenting them to the Father; His own meeting Him and worshipping in speechless love that blessed face; His own meeting each other in the ecstasy of God's own love. Let us wait, long for, and love the appearing of our Lord and Heavenly Bridegroom. Tender love to Him and tender love to each other is the true and only bridal spirit.

I fear greatly that this is sometimes forgotten. A beloved brother in Christ was speaking about the expectancy of faith as being the true sign of the bride. I ventured to express a doubt. An unworthy bride, about to be married to a prince, might only be thinking of the position and the riches that she will receive. The expectancy of faith might be strong, but true love may be utterly lacking. It is love that defines the bridal spirit. It is not when we are most occupied with prophetic subjects, but when in humility and love we draw close to our Lord and His disciples, that we occupy the bride's place. Jesus refuses to accept our love unless it extends to His disciples. Waiting for His coming means waiting for the coming manifestation of the unity of the body, so seek now to maintain that unity in humility and love. Those who love the most are the most prepared for Christ to come. Showing love to each other is the life and beauty of His bride, the church.

And how are we to do this? Beloved child of God, if you want to learn the right way to wait for His Son from heaven, live even now waiting on God in heaven. Remember how Jesus lived, always waiting on God. He could do nothing of Himself. It was God who made "the captain of their salvation perfect through suffering" before exalting Him (Hebrews 2:10).It is God alone who can give you the deep spiritual life of one who is truly waiting for His Son: wait on God for it. Waiting for Christ Himself is so different from waiting for things that may come to pass! The latter any Christian can do; the former God must work in you every day by the Holy Spirit. Therefore, all you who wait on God, wait for His Son from heaven in the bridal spirit of love. And you who wait for the Bridegroom, wait on God continually to reveal His Son in you.

The revelation of Christ in us, as it is given to those who wait on God, is the true preparation for the full revelation of Christ in glory. It is the mystery made known, "Christ in you, the hope of glory" (Colossians 1:27).

"My soul, wait only on God!"

Personal Reflection

Day 29

For the Promise of the Father

"He commanded them not to depart from Jerusalem,
but to wait for the Promise of the Father."—Acts 1:4

In studying the saints in Jerusalem at the time of Christ's birth,
Simeon and Anna, we noted that the redemption they waited
for has come. Yet the call to wait on God is no less urgent now
than it was then. We wait for the full revelation in us of what
came to them, what they could scarcely comprehend. This is also
true about waiting for the Promise of the Father. In one sense,
the fulfillment can never come again as it came at Pentecost. In
another sense, a sense as real as with the first disciples, we daily
need to wait for the Father to fulfill His Promise in us.

The Holy Spirit is not a person distinct from the Father in
the way two persons on earth are distinct. The Father and the
Spirit are never without or separate from each other: The Father
is always in the Spirit; the Spirit works nothing but only as the
Father works in Him. Each moment the same Spirit that is in us
is in God too. And the person who is most full of the Spirit will be
the first to wait on God most earnestly, to even more fully fulfill
His promise, and to be strengthened with might through His
Spirit in the inner man (Ephesians 3:16). The Spirit in us is not
simply a power at our disposal. Nor is the Spirit an independent
power, acting apart from the Father and the Son. The Spirit is *the
real living presence and the power of the Father working in us*. Therefore,
it is those of us who know that the Spirit is in us who will wait on
the Father for the full revelation and experience of the Spirit's
indwelling, for Him to increase and abound more and more.

We see this in the apostles. They were filled with the Spirit at Pentecost. Not long after, Peter and John were arrested. Upon returning from the Council of Jerusalem where they had been forbidden to preach, they prayed for boldness to speak in Jesus' name. A second coming down of the Holy Spirit was the Father's fresh fulfillment of His promise (Acts 4).

In Samaria, through Philip's preaching and healing miracles, many believed and were baptized and the whole city was filled with joy. Then Peter and John arrived and prayed for these new believers, that the Father would once again fulfill the promise, "and they received the Holy Spirit" (Acts 1:17). Later it happened again to the waiting company in Cornelius' house, who said, "We are all present before God" (Acts 10:33). So, too, it was when the disciples prayed and fasted, that the promise of the Father was fulfilled afresh, and the leading of the Spirit was given from heaven: "Now separate to Me Barnabas and Saul for the work to which I have called them" (Acts 13:3).

In his letter to the Ephesians, Paul prays for those who have been "sealed with the Holy Spirit of promise," that God would grant them "the spirit of wisdom and revelation." And further, that He would grant them, out of "the riches of His glory," the exceeding greatness of His power, ... according to the working of His mighty power" (Ephesians 1:15-19).

The Spirit given at Pentecost was not a something that God parted with in heaven and sent away out of heaven to earth. God does not, cannot, give away anything in that way. When He gives grace or strength or life, He gives it by giving Himself to work it—it is all inseparable from God Himself. This is also true of the Holy Spirit. He is God, present and working in us. We can count on the Holy Spirit working with unceasing power, but only if we, praising Him for what we have, wait without ceasing for the Father's promise to be fulfilled with even more power.

What new meaning and promise this gives to our life of waiting! It teaches us always to remain where the disciples tarried, at the footstool of God's throne. It reminds us how helpless they were to face their enemies, or to preach to Christ's enemies, before they were endued with power. We, too, can only be strong in the life of faith, or in the work of love, as we stay in direct communication with God and Christ, and as they maintain the life of the Spirit in us. It assures us that the omnipotent God will, through the glorified Christ, work in us a power that can bring to pass things unexpected, things impossible. Think of what the church would be able to do if her individual members learned to live their lives waiting on God, and if together, with all of self and the world sacrificed in the fire of love, they united in waiting with one accord for the promise of the Father, once so gloriously fulfilled, but still unexhausted.

Come and let each of us be still in the presence of the inconceivable grandeur of this prospect: The Father is waiting to fill the church with the Holy Spirit. And, let each of us say: *He is willing to fill me.* In this posture of faith, let there come over the soul a hush and a holy fear, as it waits in stillness to be filled. And let there come into the soul a deep joy, in the hope of a fresh fulfillment of the Father's Promise.

"My soul, wait only on God!"

Personal Reflection

Day 30

Waiting Continually

"So you, by the help of your God, return; observe mercy
and justice, and wait on your God continually."
—Hosea 12:6

Continuity is an essential element of life. Interrupt the
heartbeat for a single hour in a man and life is lost, he
is dead. Continuity, unbroken and ceaseless, is also essential
to a healthy Christian life. Every moment, God wants me to
be and waits to make me what is well pleasing in His sight;
and every moment I want to be and wait on Him to reveal
what He expects of me. If waiting on God is the essence of
true religion, then maintaining a spirit of entire dependence
must be continuous. The call of God to "wait on your God
continually" must be accepted and obeyed.

This waiting continually is indeed a necessity. To those
who are content with a nominal Christian life, it may seem a
luxury, as something beyond what is essential to being a good
Christian. But all those who want more of God feel the need,
and so they pray: "Lord, make me as holy as a pardoned sinner
can be made! Keep me as near to You as it is possible for me
to be! Fill me as full of your love as You are willing to do!"
They have come to understand that there can be no unbroken
fellowship with God, no full abiding in Christ, no victory over
sin, and no readiness for service without waiting continually on
the Lord.

This waiting continually is possible to do. Many think that with the duties of life it is out of the question. They cannot always be thinking of God. Even when they might try to, they forget. They do not understand that it is a matter of the heart, not the mind. It is a matter of what the heart is full of, what occupies it, even when the mind is otherwise engaged. A mother's heart will be filled continuously with intense love and longing for a sick child, even though pressing business requires her attention elsewhere. When *the heart* has learned how entirely powerless it is to bring forth any good; when it has learned how surely and truly God will keep it; when it has, in despair of itself, accepted God's promise to do for it the impossible, only then does it learn to rest in God. And, in the middle of occupations and temptations, it can wait continually.

This waiting is a promise. God's commands are all enablers; gospel precepts are all promises. All are revelations of what our God will do for us. When first you begin waiting on God, it is with frequent intermission and failure. But as you continue to wait, believe God is watching over you in love and secretly strengthening you in it. There are times when waiting seems a waste of time, but it is not so. Waiting, even in darkness, is unconscious advance; because this is God you are waiting on and He is always at work in you. God, who calls you to wait on Him, sees your feeble efforts, and works His will in you. Your spiritual life is not your own work; just as you did little to begin it, you can do little to continue it. The Holy Spirit, who has begun the work in you of waiting upon God, will enable you to wait continually.

Waiting continually will be met and rewarded by God Himself working continually. We are coming to the end of our meditations. If only you and I might learn this one lesson: God must, God will work continually. He is at work continually; our awareness of it is only hindered by our unbelief. He who by

His Spirit teaches us to wait continually, will also bring us to experience how, as the Everlasting One, His work never ceases. In the love and the life and the work of God there can be no break, no interruption.

Do not limit God in this by thoughts of what may be expected. Simply fix your eyes on this one truth: In His very nature, God, as the only Giver of life, *cannot do otherwise than every moment work in His child.* Do not look only at the one side: "If I wait continually, God will work continually." No, look at the other side: place God first and say, "God works continually, every moment I may wait on Him continually." Take time until the vision of your God working continually, without one moment's intermission, fills your being. Your waiting continually will then come of itself. Full of trust and joy, the holy habit of the soul will be, "On You I wait *all the day*" (Psalm 25:5). The Holy Spirit will always keep you waiting.

"My soul, wait only on God!"

Personal Reflection

Day 31

Only on God

"My soul, wait silently for God alone, for my expectation
is from Him. He only is my rock and my salvation."
—Psalm 62:5-6

I t is possible to be waiting continually on God, but not
waiting only on Him; there may be other secret confidences
intervening and preventing the blessing that was expected.
And so the word *only* must come to throw its light on the path
to the fullness and certainty of blessing. "My soul, wait silently
for God alone. He *only* is my Rock."

Yes, wait only on God. There is only one God, only one
source of life and happiness for the heart. You desire to be
good, but as Jesus said: "No one is good but One, that is, God"
(Matthew 19:17). There is no possible goodness but what is
received directly from Him. You have sought to be holy, but as
Hannah said: "No one is holy like the Lord, for there is none
besides You" (1 Samuel 2:2). There is no holiness but what the
Spirit of holiness every moment breathes into you. You long to
live and work for God and His kingdom, for the lost and their
salvation. Hear what Isaiah says: "The Everlasting God, the
Lord, the Creator of the ends of the earth, [He alone] neither
faints nor is weary…. He gives power to the weak, and to those
who have no might He increases strength…. But those who
wait on the Lord shall renew their strength" (Isaiah 40:28-31).
He alone has the power; He only is our Rock; He alone is holy.

Clearly, the admonition is to wait only on God. You will not find many who will help you in this practice of waiting on God. You will be encouraged to trust in churches and doctrines, in schemes and plans, in means of grace and divine appointments. So, remember, "My soul, wait only on God." His most sacred appointments become a snare when trusted in. The bronze serpent becomes Nehushtan, the ark and the temple a vain confidence. Let the Living God alone, no one and nothing but He, be your hope.

"My soul, wait only on God." Eyes and hands and feet and mind may be intently engaged in the duties of life, but may your soul wait only on God. You are an immortal spirit, created not for this world but for eternity and for God. Realize your destiny, enjoy your privilege, and wait only on God. And do not allow an interest in theological studies or religious practices to deceive you; these activities very often take the place of waiting upon God. May your soul, your inmost being, with all its power, wait only on God. God is for you, you are for God; wait only on Him.

Beware of your two great enemies—the World and Self. Beware lest any earthly satisfaction or enjoyment, however innocent it appears, keeps you from saying, "I will go to the altar of God, to God, my exceeding joy" (Psalm 43:4). Remember and study what Jesus says about denying self: "If anyone desires to come after Me, let him deny himself" (Matthew 16:24). As Gerhard Tersteegen, the German theologian, wrote: "The saints deny themselves in everything." Pleasing oneself in little things only serves to strengthen self, so that it asserts itself in greater things. Wait only on God; let Him be your only salvation and your only desire.

Say continually and with an undivided heart, "From Him comes my salvation, He only is my Rock and my salvation; He is my defense; I shall not be greatly moved" (Psalm 62:1-2).

Whatever your spiritual or temporal need may be, whatever the desire or prayer of your heart, whatever your connection with God's work in the church or the world, in solitude or in the rush of the world, in public worship or in other gatherings of the saints: "My soul, wait only on God." Let your expectations be from Him alone. HE ONLY IS YOUR ROCK.

"My soul, wait only on God." Never forget the two foundational truths on which this blessed waiting rests. If you are ever inclined to think this "waiting only" is too hard or too high, these two truths will bring you back at once. They are simply: your absolute helplessness and the absolute sufficiency of your God.

Consider deeply the sinfulness of all that is of self, and do not allow self its say in anything for even one moment. Consider deeply your utter impotence to change what is evil in yourself, or to bring forth anything that is spiritually good. Consider deeply your dependency as creature on God your Creator, receiving from Him every moment what you need. Delve deeper still into His covenant of redemption, with His promise to restore more gloriously than ever what you had lost, and by His Son and His Spirit to give you unceasingly His divine presence and power. Just wait on your God continually and only.

"My soul, wait only on God." No words can express, no mind conceive, the riches of the glory of this mystery of the Father and of Christ. Our God, in the infinite tenderness and omnipotence of His love, waits to be our Life and Joy. Oh, my soul, may I no longer need to repeat the words, "Wait only on God," but let all that is in me arise and sing: "Truly my soul waits on God. On You do I wait all the day."

"My soul, wait only on God!"

Personal Reflection

Lives Changed by Waiting on God

My *Waiting on God* has brought subtle yet significant transformation, not only in the lives of individuals in our church, but also in the culture of how we follow Jesus and love those around us. Through the simple yet challenging practice of waiting on God, a whole world of faith and intimacy is unlocked with the Father. Take it one day at a time and see what God will bring about as you wait on Him.

Chris Millar
Lead Pastor, The Well

What a journey of faith, hope and love. *Waiting on God*, this is not a concept it is a movement, a movement of God waiters, to which I have the humble joy of belonging. It began on a helpless hopeless morning. The congregation I pastor and other ministries that I so lovingly serve, they too were at the end of their proverbial ropes. I was led by the Holy Spirit to finally use the Waiting on God journal that my friend Colin Millar introduced to me more than once. In fact, he have given me two books in the past, but quite frankly I was too busy to wait. Upon my journey of investing time in reading Brother Andrew Murray's devotional material, I begin to weep as I read the compelling words of waiting on God. I invited my congregation and other ministries to join me in a 31 day experience. It has been almost a whole year that most of us have been on this journey together, every day. The results have been a renewed faith and an absolute expectation of hope and love that is above and beyond all I can ever pray for or imagine. Because of this journey of waiting on God hundreds and maybe even thousands have experienced this awesome spiritual journey of waiting on God. Every minister has the responsibility to teach God's people to wait on God!

Pastor Rickie Bradshaw
Founder of Greater Houston Prayer Council

I have served on the mission field both globally and locally for over 30 years. During a great transition time in my life, Colin Millar met with me for prayer. We waited on God, then he read aloud to me from Day 27 of the book. We prayed, wept, and laughed at the pure presence of the Father. Wherever you are in your spiritual journey, I greatly encourage you to read and practice *Waiting on God* for 31 days. Only you can choose to begin this transformation of the power of the practice of waiting for the Father who waits for you.

Marsha T.
Global Pastor of Missions and Movements

For many years I have read the Bible daily and through the Bible yearly, I have prayed in earnest and frequently. Then I read *Waiting on God* and found that listening for His supplies (Day 4), His instructions (Day 5), and His counsel (Day 15) has deepened my relationship with Him. Sometimes relationships can become one sided; one person does all the talking, taking, and directing. Yes, God wants to hear from me, but also, He wants me to listen and hear from Him. May my life be a testimony of living life His way by waiting on Him and following Him, not doing life my way but His way.

Debbie B.
Intercessor and Bible Teacher

Waiting on God impacted my ministry as both an intercessor and intercessory leader as I realized that in serious intercession – whether about issues on a personal, family, church, city, country, or continental level – waiting on God is an important component of intercession. In the ministry of Luke 10 Transformation (L-10-T), we aim to get all believers in the world to pray, connect with not-yet believers, care for the needs of people around them, and share Jesus every day everywhere – thereby becoming walking disciples making disciples.

By waiting on God, we realized that integrating waiting on God into each part of the L-10-T disciple's lifestyle brings greater effectiveness, a closer walk with God, more disciples, and greater joy and peace to the practitioners. A massive impact on the ministry!

Willem J.
Founder of Luke 10 Transformation

To quote this amazing book, "God longs to reveal Himself, to fill us up with Himself. *Waiting on God* provides time for Him to come to us in His own way and with divine power." Oh, how He has filled me since I have been practicing waiting on Him.

My life will never be the same! I wake up each morning excited to enjoy time in His presence and to feel His great pleasure as I simply wait on Him in the quiet. I fall more and more in love with our magnificent Savior each and every time I wait on Him. My family will never be the same! Since starting this practice, we have returned to being in fellowship with other believers at church, my children have expressed a desire to be baptized, and the atmosphere in our home has become more joy-filled and peaceful.

Amy S.
Stay-at-Home Mother of Two

When we began our waiting on God journey, my wife and I were in the middle of a huge transition. We had sold our home in Kingwood, Texas, and had been waiting for our new home to close in Livingston, Texas. We had been in transitional housing for four months at that time, living in a basement apartment. We were exhausted and not sure what the future looked like.

I had put on a considerable amount of weight. I was not sleeping well, and my body hurt at night. I had no energy. I felt at a dead end in my health, my ministry, and my life's purpose.

When I heard about *Waiting on God*, I had been a man of prayer for 40 years. What was this all about? I had a lot of doubts and questions.

Then I waited. I started my church waiting. And though I cannot explain it, my life took off. House closed and we moved in, we began a new way of eating and I lost 55 pounds. We started a School of Leadership Development that drew in 44 paying students with the desire to lead in the business world, in the political realm, and in ministry.

The church grew. We have gone from one to two services and are working on planting a church about 45 minutes from our own as we prepare for more growth and expansion. We have given thousands of dollars to missions all over the world and are currently building two churches, one in northern India and the other in South Africa.

All glory to God! All this has been in the waiting and not in our activity.

Mike Hooper
Lead Pastor, Church on the Lake

Thank you for your commitment to teach all of us to wait on the Lord daily! I'm experiencing a new normal of something related to my waiting on the Lord and it is wonderful. The more I intentionally sow His Word into my mind and heart, I'm finding that when I pause to wait on the Lord, like bubbling fountains from the deep, His Word is coming up. Like rivers of living water, it flows through my mind and the Holy Spirit and I have a wonderful time. He may highlight one particular verse or many, but either way I am finding that the more I sow the Word of God into my heart, He is bringing fruitful harvest when I wait on Him.

Amy Stoehr
Prayer Igniter

Throughout my time of learning to wait on God, I've gained so much insight into the way of Jesus. The simple practice of waiting on God to speak to me has opened my spiritual ears in a brand-new way. I'm hearing Him daily and letting Him lead me in my motherhood journey now more than ever. I've started waiting instead of reacting when my four girls seem to be running in every direction. When it feels as if things are spinning out of control I simply stop, press pause, and I feel Holy Spirit invade the moment. I've seen a great change in my patience, in their response to my requests, and in our daily interactions. Our normal busyness is still present but, thanks to *Waiting on God*, I'm approaching our schedule and the chaos so differently now. It's also impacted my relationship with my phone, friends, and the things I commit my time to. It's upsetting I didn't take this practice to heart sooner, but NO ONE who waits on the Lord will be put to shame.

Amy Nickle
Mother

IGNITING
PRAYER
ACTION

Made in United States
North Haven, CT
03 October 2023

42290136R00088